THE
THIRD EYE

ALSO BY GIAN KUMAR

Know Thyself

Think from the Heart, Love from the Mind

The Ultimate Reality

Spiritual Power: Being & Becoming – Volume 1

Spiritual Power: The Mask of the Absolute – Volume 2

Spiritual Power: God and Beyond – Volume 3

THE THIRD EYE

AWAKENING
YOUR TRUE SELF

GIAN KUMAR

HAY HOUSE

Carlsbad, California • New York City
London • Sydney • New Delhi

Published in the United Kingdom by:
Hay House UK Ltd, The Sixth Floor, Watson House,
54 Baker Street, London W1U 7BU
Tel: +44 (0)20 3927 7290; Fax: +44 (0)20 3927 7291; www.hayhouse.co.uk

Published in India by:
Hay House Publishers India, Muskaan Complex, Plot No.3, B-2,
Vasant Kunj, New Delhi 110 070
Tel: (91) 11 4176 1620; Fax: (91) 11 4176 1630; www.hayhouse.co.in

Text © Gian Kumar, 2021

The moral rights of the author have been asserted.

The information given in this book should not be treated as a substitute for professional medical advice; always consult a medical practitioner. Any use of information in this book is at the reader's discretion and risk. Neither the author nor the publisher can be held responsible for any loss, claim or damage arising out of the use, or misuse, of the suggestions made, the failure to take medical advice or for any material on third-party websites.

A catalogue record for this book is available from the British Library.

Tradepaper ISBN: 978-1-78817-842-6

To the greatest of the great, Sage Ashtavakra,
who enlightened us on what you are about to read.

CONTENTS

'Man has many scriptures, but none are comparable to the Gita of Ashtavakra. Before it the Vedas pale, the Upanishads are a mere whisper. Even the Bhagavad Gita does not have the mere majesty found in the Ashtavakra Samhita—it is simply unparalleled.'

—Osho*

*Chandra Mohan Jain, popularly known as Osho, or Acharya Rajneesh (1931–1990), was an Indian guru, mystic, and founder of the Rajneesh movement.

INTRODUCTION

$\mathcal{T}$ODAY, WE FIND THE SUBJECT OF SPIRITUALISM ALL jumbled up in mysticism and mythology primarily because most of us are not patient and do not put in serious effort to study and understand this subject independently. With blind beliefs, we keep ranting and chanting without making any attempt to apprehend the fundamentals of this subject. We restrict ourselves to its outer edge, blindly following, gossiping, and singing praises of our deities and of celebrities commonly dressed in monkish style. We ignore the in-depth message of this subject or the essence of its teachings, which time and again tells us: All you require is to explore and discover your true self, the rest follows effortlessly.

The higher knowledge is that of 'self-knowledge', the true self, which is not our body and mind. The lower one in our subject is that of the phenomenal world. To understand this complex know-how of 'who we are', we will need perseverance, multiple readings, concentration, and consistency of those words, sentences, and meanings, which are repeated time and again. It is required for gaining that clarity, which is the essence of any academic subject. Kindly read this book with an open mind to procure something different, even if the information provided does not concur with what you have been told earlier or believe in. The deep research to uncover the truth behind the nature of our reality is more to undo that rigid conditioning of our mind over centuries. Self-knowledge, I believe, is vitally important, that is, if we require, besides profits and pleasure, a balanced life with mental peace and tranquillity in this chaotic world of ours.

Our illusory existence of body and brain is fundamentally based on a temporary reality of *me*, *mine*, and *myself*. We do not seem to realize we are a unique reflection of not only the body and mind but also that of the spirit in unity and continuity. According to the subject of spiritualism, the spirit is the ultimate of *who* we actually are. It is that universal impersonal integrant contained in an individual soul, which we so liberally use but, in reality, do not bother to know what it is or what role it plays in our personal life. Our body and mind appear and disappear into that absolute constituent from where they materialize and dematerialize. However, individuality—or that uniqueness guided by the consciousness—leaves behind a certain legacy after death, the sum of our deeds for all to remember. Therefore, it is imperative for us to know what this third faculty is about because, despite all the material and social comforts, it is difficult for the mind to be at peace unless it comprehends what this conscious principle is all about.

This volume, like my other books, does not delve into supernatural beliefs and fables, nor does it revolve around religion. It strictly adheres to the subject at hand in total seriousness and demands your full attention while reading the same, but of course, with a free and open mind. I reiterate, spiritual concepts are repeatedly explained in different words to impel the message for that lucidity, which is the actual ethos of this subject.

There is no such thing as *moksha*, self-realization, or becoming absolute in pure consciousness while living in our confined space and time with an independent name and gender. The body and mind are designed and restricted to experience duality, say that of God and the devil in relativity with opposites for the spiritual self to undergo a transitory material manifestation. You just cannot ignore any; you can only simply surf between the two. The spirit, on one hand, is forever enlightened and realized, whereas the body and mind get the opportunity to experience and realize how and in what way to tread a path towards higher consciousness. Like a tightrope walker, you are to balance that pole with your head held high and celebrate your material life with your third eye open.

Life cyclically moves, like all other forms of energy, for that evolution—from one beyond to another. It creates a certain *becoming-ness* from its conscious and subconscious experiences where death indicates only a new beginning. Energy vibrates and moves in a circular pattern where there is no beginning nor end—like the planets or the seasons— circling around, eventually disintegrating as dark matter or dark energy, which we refer to as *Shunyata* (nothingness). The universe, according to science, consists only of energy comprising around 5 per cent in matter and consciousness and the huge leftover—95 per cent—as dark matter and energy.

In the subatomic level, matter and consciousness are just vibrations resonating and synchronizing in various frequencies from their respective quantum fields. Furthermore, energy tends to move randomly in entropy like in the case of thoughts—creating, destroying, and recreating to expand and effectuate. It requires aware-conscious energy to stabilize, evolve, and transform. The dark matter and energy, on the other hand, represent nothing but sheer bliss in equilibrium.

Once the mind comes to know with clarity that its true master is a state of impersonal *being-ness* as the spirit, all imaginations of personal gods as well as that of the personal 'I' disappear. Only human minds have this ability to comprehend the cosmos and utilize the potentiality behind the assertion of 'Thou Art That'. After clearly attaining self-knowledge, the brain acknowledges the universe as a unified field of reality in continuity, which remains potent, latent, and acquiescent in Shunyata. However, when this noumenal energy vibrates and collides, all sorts of phenomenal attributes in the forms of matter and consciousness come to life, which endures for a while before yielding to that dormant state of universal aware energy. This has been clarified in detail later in this book.

Of all those transitory features representing matter and consciousness, ranging from the subatomic particles to the stars, the human mind has been ascribed as the potential divine. It is knowable through its phenomenal attributes, which embraces both the creator and its creation as one. It is attributed in this manner due to the presence of this supreme energy, the spirit, which we also refer to as awareness, something that makes it possible for the universe to exist. Everything unfolds and exists *only* because we are aware of what we perceive, otherwise, it is impossible.

Awareness is that *essence* of perception, which permits all possibilities to collapse into their actuality. This eternal force of energy embedded in the mind remains absolute and non-dual, whereas the transient field of energies—in the forms of body and mind—disappear and dissipate into the infinite expanse of nothingness. What ultimately remains is dark matter and energy, which envelops this universe, of which, as of now, we have no clue.

Therefore, what we have is unitary absolute energy, the ultimate substratum, the ground substance and the essence of both dual and non-dual existence. It exists as it is, indicating that nothing is everything. The nature of this pure, intelligent energy expresses its being-ness from its aliveness through awareness in the form of life. In living creatures, all that is visible and knowable is not from what we see or hear, but after we become *aware* of what we perceive. The spirit of awareness as supreme energy remains passive and dormant, not aware of itself. It is that phenomenal mind, which is capable of awakening this noumenal spirit in order to make its mind aware and conscious, confirming the postulation. Creator and the creation are one and the same.

Spirit pertaining to our subject is that state of being-ness or awareness residing non-locally outside the limitations of space and time, ushering the conscious principle to activate our mind and making it alive. It remains dormant until the mind becomes aware and conscious to conceive what it perceives. The spirit is not aware of itself but through alert observation; it is the mind, which becomes aware and after that conscious to experience life in relativity with the duality of opposites—good/bad, positive/negative, truth/lie, etc.

Furthermore, there is no 'this' or 'that' in our universe or any 'past', 'present', and 'future'. What exists is an absolute form of constant energy in unity and continuity, representing only 'this' in the eternal now, the way it is, in this spaceless, timeless, and limitless exhibition of the infinite constant source. The eternal presence is only of dark energy, which signifies that from this *nothingness* emerges that transitory *something*, from subatomic particles to stars, which becomes *everything* for us, while we exist in our material life.

The human mind has been distinguished as the potential divine due to the reason that the spirit—in the form of absolute aware energy—resides within the soul, empowering our minds to comprehend all that exists in this universe is one and not two. In spiritualism, we refer the same as *Brahman* (spirit) and in quantum physics as energy. Moreover, the nature of reality exists in two separate domains—one within *space and time* in physicality and the other outside, in the realm of aware conscious energy.

We, as the spirit, merely exist as waves of aware energy emerging as that force to create something through its field of consciousness and return to its source. Without the apprehension of this marvel, the purpose of life goes in vain; otherwise, we continue to endure the vicious cycle of pleasure and pain.

When we refer to transient forms like matter and consciousness, these are just illusions of the mind. What ultimately prevails is explained in the wave-function theory in quantum physics. We are probable waves of energy, which collapse or condense into particles in mass only after being *observed* from the mind. Because, without observation, nothing can be verified, and it is that observation from the mind, which becomes aware and, after that, conscious of every perception. Meaning, awareness is the ground (noumenal) of all beings, and the mind is a phenomenon of this supreme energy.

Quantum science further tells us that matter, radiation, and energy surround us; the entire universe emerges from this infinite expanse and, eventually, returns to the same. From the above, we assume there is no eternal or immortal life—these are mere rotary cycles of different attributes of energy, which dissipate into the same infinitude of dark energy or, say, into that nothing. Thus, after observing through all our instruments, matter and consciousness sum up to only 5 per cent, and the remainder is referred to as the dark matter and dark energy, of which more is unknown than known.

The ancient sages declared that out of this dark emptiness, Shunyata, everything emerges but only after your mind sees and observes through its witnessing self, which we refer to as the soul. Within the physical form, the creator (spirit) activates within the soul of a living being, a section of the mind. Meaning, an individual soul contains and entraps the absolute aware energy performing as the *witnessing observer* until the physical form exists. The eternal spirit of aware absolute energy does not require any moksha or liberation from any other force or field of energy. It exists, as it is, radiating through consciousness in all living creatures.

Now, if the mind wishes to enhance its degree of consciousness, it is required to free this spirit, imprisoned amid illusory identifications and attachments of its incessant desires. In such a case, the mind does not accept any doership, because when we let go this feeling of doership, we become unaffected and uninvolved, and our true self as the witness/ spirit transpires, which is aloof and independent from the body and mind. A mere onlooker of every thought and deed. With the result, all three—the body, mind, and soul— become dispassionate and sensitive to all that is around with no likes or dislikes. We, in turn, as the spirit, become free from bindings in attachments to this or that. Meaning, the mind becomes proactively sensitive to all that exists and not sentimentally reactive for a select few. It exudes love with humility for all as one.

It is that thinking mind, which emotionally binds both the spirit and the body through desires, identifications, and attachments to worldly objects—consciously as well as subconsciously. Desire is that strong force, which suppresses the actual self, the soul from what the mind thinks, believes, and experiences. You, as the witness (*Sakshi*), the presence of that spirit—if and when awakened—have this potential to shake off the mind-body entrapment and stay aloof by being a dispassionate *witness-er* through its soul. You, then, have full command over your mind and flow freely to enjoy that freedom with mental peace and tranquillity, which we all yearn for.

This volume lays stress upon going beyond the precepts, techniques, and methods of spirituality prescribed and conceptualized by the mind. If we wish to awaken our spirit, the mind is required to enter deep into the realm of that witnessing self, beyond thinking, experiencing, or any doing from the mind. The 'observer effect' in science also signifies that an observer influences the observed reality. Spiritual practices are more of applied psychology to tame and discipline the mind, making it mindful. All such methods undertaken by the mind will travel only towards the periphery of the core but not the centre—the spirit.

You are supposed to effortlessly go beyond spirituality and enter into that centre and awaken that soul containing the spirit. Meaning, go over and above your cognitive senses and not be a slave of your mind. Sensual inputs fundamentally survive and sustain via thoughts only of the past and future. The spirit proacts spontaneously in the present before any cognitive reactions can take place. This volume will take you beyond that realm, where you are not the observer, observing the observed, but a sheer observation (witness) in the form of absolute non-dual energy. You may have to read every extrapolation more than once to capture the essence of what it conveys, but read with a free and open mind to go beyond that ultimate knowledge of who, what, and how you are, and discover the nature of the ultimate reality—one without a second.

I repeat, all thoughts, efforts, and actions remain under the purview of the cognitive senses. Meditation, yoga, Zen, vipassana, T'ai chi, etc., are physical and mental efforts applied by the senses through a motivated or desirous mind to control that very mind, which is impossible. The mind can never be reached through the mind, you need to go beyond to comprehend the unknown, the spirit. These aforementioned exercises are helpful as therapy and have substantial physical as well as mental benefits for the body and the brain.

The brain is that hardware and mind is its operating system processing and transmitting through neural pathways the information that it receives. The spirit on the other hand is that absolute aware energy entrapped in the individualized soul. You shall read a lot more on the role that a soul plays checking and guiding the mind as and when the mind goes astray through its individual degree of self-consciousness. Because, after all, it is that conscious principle, that wakefulness, which activates and makes the mind alive on all that it perceives.

The mind, even after being activated, remains reckless in its thoughts, randomly functioning through its subconscious section in an unconscious manner. The subject of spiritualism conveys that it is not possible to control the mind for long; it is designed to run on its own from its subconscious section. Even if you try, your material thoughts will bounce back in spite of all those psychic efforts, methods, and practices mentioned above into its fundamental desirous nature in ego-consciousness, merely to gossip: 'I do meditation, yoga etc.'

The spirit is that transcendent seated within the mind, which requires just awakening with zero practices, and this volume will tell you how in detail. You need to go beyond the conscious and the subconscious, deep into that *unconscious* zone of what the spiritualists refer as the superconscious section. In this section of the mind, cognition is absent, so nothing disturbs the serenity, solitude, and silence. It is in this superconscious realm the spirit resides, which you will gradually understand on your own and further experience, and not because somebody says so.

Please do not try to take shortcuts or blindly follow those who wear robes and turbans, or for that matter, those who do not wear ample clothing, living in various spiritual and religious institutions across our country. You must first endeavour to understand, after making the mind open and free from your conditioned, rigid, and prejudiced nature, engrained with ancient *shlokas* (poems in Sanskrit) in exhausted blind beliefs ranging over thousands of years—genetically as well as psychologically. The time has come; it is ripe for you to go beyond. This book is allocated to that unconscious section of the mind, the state of superconsciousness, where the senses of the brain have little ground to play.

Opening your mind to this exclusive subject of spiritualism is neither straightforward nor conclusive. It is a continuous approach of unfolding your true self, maturing into an intelligent level of understanding as you go deeper and deeper into the subject. Ashtavakra Gita, compared to other scriptures or philosophies, is not well known, for it has no fables, fantasies, or any supernatural mystical or mythical implications. It is a short, compact, well-knit treatise clarifying rationally how to live without any philosophical or psychological undertones.

Chapter 1

THE STAR IN ONESELF

*'For a star to be born, there is one thing that
must happen: a gaseous nebula must collapse. So
collapse. Crumble. This is not your destruction.
This is your birth.'*

—Anonymous

WHILE SITTING DOWN TO WRITE THIS VOLUME, I OBSERVED all sorts of thoughts ruminating the mind, appearing obscure. As usual, I was multitasking—thinking not of what is at hand but of other matters. I consciously woke up from this unconscious sleep, became attentive, and only after that the random thoughts started disappearing. Osho explained this phenomenon aptly when he said, 'It takes a little time to create a gap between the witness and the mind . . . as you become more deeply rooted in witnessing and thoughts start disappearing. You are, but the mind is utterly empty. That's the moment of enlightenment.'

Now, the question arises, how do we create this gap between the witness and the mind. The subject of spiritualism has prevailed in India for over five thousand years when different seers during this period proclaimed *Aham Brahmasmi.* Meaning, we are that spiritual conscious energy; the body and mind do not constitute the true self. Everything that exists is not of what we see or hear from our senses but of what we are *aware of.* It is not because of the physical being but because of the presence of that being-ness.

Therefore, all that the mind sees and deciphers through its knowingness occurs only because we are a witness to that occurrence. It is due to that witnessing or observing, which makes the mind, first, aware and, after that, conscious to compare and infer what it sees. It is that aware/conscious principle that makes this possibility into an actuality of all that exists in this universe. Again, it is this aware conscious energy, which we generally ignore, as a result, we live in a world of disorder and despair. None of us is concerned to make serious efforts to know and understand our true spiritual self. We are merely fixated by the limited mind in a vicious cycle of pleasure and pain depending upon information provided by others.

We all know that the universe encompasses infinite space containing matter and energy, but unless we are aware of them, the possibility for the universe to exist does not arise. The presence of our awareness is that source and the force, which actualizes all possibilities radiating a field of consciousness in our brain to experience and realize what the mind perceives. Thus, awareness precedes more as an abstract state of being-ness rather than be measured and concretized. Meaning, the 'I, me, and self' are all misleading. There is no permanent unchanging self; we temporarily exist with an 'I' in a physical state and eternally in an *I-less* state of being-ness that is unrelated to any space, time, or causation. Whenever we designate any physical object with a name and description, whether a human god or any living or non-living object, it is more of an illusion as dictated both by science and spiritualism. Because when we observe any objective matter in the most fundamental or subatomic level, it is composed merely of interchangeable particles and waves of energy.

Likewise, our minds are conditioned and prejudiced to what we think and believe. We wrongly presume the mind and its thoughts to be that true self. Thoughts emerge from the memory connected to the past and projects that information into future thoughts. However, what exists before and after thoughts is awareness, that *is-ness,* which is always present in the eternal now, from which every concept—including the past and the future—arises. Those who have true knowledge about the real essence of this *being-ness* understand that *I-am, I-was,* and *I-will be* is merely superimposed on that selfless waves of aware energy without an 'I', where there are zero concepts, conceiving the conceivability. It is just the presence of the substratum of all that exists in an unchanging state of nothingness.

The simple reason being, the body and mind on their own do not feel or know anything; all-knowingness emerges from the inert nature of energy possessing this attribute of being aware. All other forms of energy from nano to nuclear are transient. The one and only permanent existence is awareness. It is that ultimate, which exists before, during, and after all matter and consciousness, authorizing the perception of all transient existences. Hence, the universe unfolds in the ambit of being-ness, in front of our eyes and the mind, but only after we are aware. *Awareness is that essence of perception.*

The subject of spiritualism explores the true permanent nature of your being-ness: *'Tat Tvam Asi* (Thou Art That)'. This bold dictum declares: I am that ultimate, I am Brahman, I am that formless spirit of awareness radiating a field of conscious energy, which is beyond the physical form of 'you' and 'I'. Brahman refers to that absolute and ultimate cosmic reality, derived from the Sanskrit root *brh* (to expand, evolve, and effectuate while remaining constant and indivisible). It refers to that constant ingredient, which exists on its own, not requiring any support but manifesting itself contrastingly in divergent temporary forms.

If we can explore, define, and clearly understand this truth, we have conquered the mystery of life. This daring and profound doctrine is the core of our spiritual philosophy, which declares individual to be 'I', and any human god has no meaning. If we wish to be free from all identifications and attachments of name, gender, religion, etc., we first need to comprehend that the creator is that creation, subsuming all that exists as one entity and not two. What is vital to know here is: All that exists is superimposed on the one and only spirit of awareness/energy. It is the ground of all being. Only after that, you may pursue further to apprehend the true nature of your reality, which is the fundamental basis of this volume.

Life is nothing but a series of experiences. So long as the mind and body continue to experience under the guidance of the soul, life goes on. When this process stops, the mind runs amok, randomly and recklessly multitasking into this and that. In this study, you will discover the actual nature of your reality, the correct answer to the question, 'Who am I?' We are told: 'I think; therefore, I am', whereas the spirit clarifies: 'I am; therefore, the mind can think'. I am that being-ness, which is the *quintessence of perception*. The mind simply cannot deny that the universe within which all that exists is possible only after the mind becomes aware, meaning, that inner being-ness reveals the true nature of my reality.

The spirit/awareness precedes all that exists and remains eternal. Because all other existences are changeable and perishable, not remaining constant. It is only awareness, which is real, which persists before and after any creation. Everything else is only an illusion. What seems to be real is not since they are not constant and prone to change. Awareness is the only existence, which is real—consistent and persistent—that which is always there in an I-less state of free-flowing eternal universal energy.

Our being-ness, the presence of awareness, is always present in the eternal now. Whether we are awake, dreaming, or asleep, awareness is always present with what *is*. When we are sleeping, consciousness is passive; awareness remains active. Allowing everything in our body and mind to function in synchronization. Leave a question before you go to sleep and have an answer ready when you are awake. Awareness is always present to unravel the past, present, and future from which everything flows. Know you are the presence of your individual intensity of aware energy signified with the suffix of -ness as awareness. Flow spontaneously; do not resist, refrain, repel, or reign from your mind. Just flow and witness the mind with the presence of being-ness contained within an individual soul, which signifies and symbolizes an individual witness-er or that observer observing through the mind of all that is being observed.

The spirit of aware energy, unchanging and free from all bindings, identifications, and attachments. It remains changeless from childhood, through youth and old age, expanding and evolving your consciousness towards that wholeness of all that exists. To recognize this reality, you need to prepare our mind, know and understand to awaken this spirit lying dormant within. It is present in the unconscious section of your mind where thoughts are absent. The presence of this aware energy is what activates the mind and has been designated as the inner spirit—that potential divine residing within the soul. It has this ability to make the mind, first, aware, and, after that, conscious of its own body and mind, which thereafter flows in its ego, persona, identity, character, as well as self-consciousness forming your unique individuality as you mature and age.

Any study, for that matter, has two prime factors—subject and object. In our case, the *inner perception* through awareness is the subject and the *outer* consciousness perceived by the senses evaluating consciously or subconsciously from its thoughts is the objective. It is easy for anyone to say 'go into your inner self', and equally easy for followers to postulate after listening to some religious discourses to claim that they have 'become spiritual'. But this *inner self* is a highly complex subject, more to be *understood* than *experienced*. When the mind clearly understands this subject, one realizes the holistic sense and the connection between the body, mind, and spirit with respect to the physical, mental, and the spiritual.

A spiritual seeker should mentally be prepared to accept in order to distinguish between the formless spirit and the forms of body and brain. When the metaphysical spirit comes into contact with the mechanical mind, life begins. The subject in our case is awareness, the spirit being the absolute (pure and total) energy, and the objective is the role played in relativity by the mind functioning in duality. The mind separates every form of transient energy into its opposites to experience materiality in physicality in order to experience life consciously. How? When the spirit observes, the mind becomes aware and, after that, conscious of perceiving both—*the inside as well as the outside*. This means, besides observing and becoming aware of the environment, the human brain also has this ability to be self-aware, which is a process of witnessing inwards. This occurs when the mental self watches and witnesses those *inner* random thoughts; the spirit awakens making the mind realize that apart from the thinking self, there is another bigger inner Self watching all that the mind does.

However, if the mind remains ignorant about this metaphysical ability, the spirit remains dormant and passive. Life remains a flow of subconscious experiences acquiring material data unconsciously from past awareness, which is what is happening today. As you read, people are distressed with despair, depression, and despondency. Humanity is on the verge of self-destruction where billions go hungry suffering in pain so that a few can relish at their cost for the sake of wastage, pleasure, and profits.

The mind drifts through life, submerged in desires and attachments, pleasure and pain, without knowing the true meaning and purpose of life. Spiritualism equips the mind with knowledge of the inner spirit and its ability to lead the mind towards higher consciousness of knowing the true essence of life rather than overly depending upon mechanization and digital comforts. The practice of this subject is what we refer to as spirituality, which constitutes mental efforts and techniques to discipline your material ego/self towards the core presence of spiritual awareness, so that you may walk the path of life with a balanced approach.

Please remember, the *spirit* through its individual *soul* only watches and witnesses; it is the mind that feels, thinks, acts, enjoys, and experiences. Both are distinct and defined by this philosophy, and a spiritual seeker is required to comprehend the difference between the two. The concept of the abstract spirit comprising pure aware energy declaring 'Creator is the creation' has always been difficult for the masses to comprehend. For this reason, the subject of spiritualism is currently diluted and mutated with mysticism and mythological jargon in various religious and philosophical texts to accommodate and appease the masses, making it easier for them to know this subject superficially.

However, in the philosophy of spiritualism, all that manifests in the universe is one without a second; the one in many and the same one behind many are referred to as the spirit or Brahman. Clearly, we cannot even consider the Bhagavad Gita or Ramayana or even Buddha's teachings as spiritual. They are concerned more with the mindful self in dharmic efforts and actions rather than the role played by the independent spirit beyond the sphere of the mind. In short, perceptively everything is finite, but when we go deeper, the infinite non-dual dimensions are revealed. It is this I-less state of being-ness within any human self, the highest attribute of energy, which we refer to as the spirit; eternally enlightened and realized as that spiritual divine, which provides credence to the spiritual claim of 'Thou Art That'.

Spiritualism, in its true essence, is primarily concerned with awareness (subject—being-ness) and consciousness (object—*becoming-ness*), where the spirit and the consciousness both play their respective roles. Awareness manifests as a *force* of mental power in the mind and consequently materializes into its conscious *field*, undertaking all mental activities to become something materially. Both are equally relevant. The individual intensity of awareness is required to assess the true nature of bliss of that ultimate reality and consciousness, in turn, reflects the physical transitory nature of your individual mid-reality. The former is present in a *state of being-ness*, while the latter expands and evolves into your *becoming-ness*, which is consciousness.

The spirit, however, is free from all identifications and attachments because it merely flows with the power to observe without participating in any of the mind's activities. This supreme formless energy, the ultimate existence, or the spirit is considered to be that creator empowering its creation; the mind to self-awaken through self-observation. The *spirit*, though situated in the brain, is not the observer, thinker, knower, doer, experiencer, or the enjoyer . . . but only the source of observation. It comprises waves of absolute energy to make your mind aware of its unconscious activities. It is that individual soul, which is assigned as the observer. The mind becomes aware only after it is alert, and if attentive becomes conscious of all that it feels, thinks, experiences, and realizes. The moment you are not alert, the memory and intellect take over; the mind then functions as the remember-er in autopilot unconsciously from its subconscious level from past awareness.

The mind, on the other hand, is simply an operating system consuming combined thoughts of past and future from which emerges a *thinker*. This thinker provides us with a name, identity, family, gender, etc., which is provided by others. Thus, a thinker that reveals the 'I', 'me', and 'mine' is nothing but a bundle of thoughts originating from the memory—to remind you of what you physically are in the form of body, mind, and self-consciousness. It is temporary because all three are present for a finite space and time, despite the thinker giving you that feeling of infinite permanence. A thinker can never be *'you'* because you will never claim: 'I am mind or thoughts'. You will refer to your body and mind as: 'My mind, my thoughts, and my body', certifying you are beyond body and mind—the spirit revealing itself through your consciousness. It is because of being ignorant about the spirit, the body, mind, and soul constantly remain separated and unfulfilled.

On the contrary, uninvolved witnessing is the domain of the spirit and experiencing is that of the mind. The spirit perpetually remains as the transcendent, the divine supreme energy, which does not require any further awareness, experiencing, or realization by the immanent mind. Its presence is primarily to check and counter the mind before it begins to experience any sensation or situation. It makes the mind aware and conscious.

I reiterate, besides the body and the cognitive mind, which selfishly thinks in separation for its personal 'me' and 'mine', there exists another flow—waves of absolute energy—which is independent of thoughts. It is this core energy, we refer to as the spirit, which has the power to make the mind observe, awaken, attentive, and aware, and yet remains constant and total in choiceless thoughts. The presence of this aware energy is that divine within, which is connected directly to the cosmos and not to the thoughts.

The presence of awareness is the highest attribute of energy and is, thus, referred to as Aham Brahmasmi, meaning, you are that aware conscious energy—the absolute, eternal, constant, ultimate reality as the Supreme Aware Energy. It enables every phenomenal human mind to be capable of that noumenal potential of observational power, from which we are able to decipher and decode the secrets of this divine energy. The soul, nevertheless, is that midway between the personal (ego) and the transpersonal (spirit) universal energy.

Spiritualism helps to free one's mind *from all concepts* created by the finite minds and enlightens the mind towards the infinite *eternity*. It conveys that the eternal spirit within each individual is the same as the infinite absolute non-dual energy, which encompasses and subsumes all that exists in this universe.

It is when the mind is ignorant about its master, the impersonal and impartial spirit gets entrapped in unconscious activities subconsciously overtaken by the mind. The mind is that ego, or the thinking self, based on body/mind relationship that is made up of conscious and subconscious thoughts from its memory and intellect. It is that personal material self, which encounters and undergoes all dualities of life in relativity. It becomes bound with identifications and attachments to become that experiencer of what it desires.

All the knowledge of any thinker does not have any permanent existence and disappears like waves in an ocean. 'You' as the presence of that aware energy is eternally emerging from the ocean of awareness. The non-changing self will never claim 'I am the body nor a mind'. You know you are something more than the mind. It is after you manifest in the body/brain that the mind becomes conscious; otherwise, the brain is dead meat. The dissolution of consciousness is elucidated only after an awakened soul realizes with clarity that the whole universe is nothing—Shunyata—leaving behind a long list of conceptualizations formulated for acquiring knowledge for the material world.

It is only after your mind matures from its narrow thinking that it starts to move towards its true reality. You need to awaken this dormant spirit residing within the mind and make it free from the mind's cognition and self-consciousness. This can happen when your mind is free and open, and not rigid under blind beliefs . . . when you, as the spirit, are free to witness all that the mind does. It is your mind, which is under delusion, thinking itself to be that supreme when it is not and, hence, requiring moksha or liberation from worldly attachments. The spirit neither insists nor expects any liberation, say, from meditation or yogic techniques; nor does it ever desire to visit any temples or ashrams to recite any mantras or prayers. The spirit is self-luminous, which illuminates the mind through sheer observation.

Chapter 2

STILL THE MIND;
AWAKEN THAT SPIRIT

'You are the clear space of awareness, Pure and still,
In whom there is no birth, no activity, No "I".
You are one and the same. You cannot change or die.'

—Paramahansa Yogananda, Ashtavakra Gita (5.13)

LET ME TAKE YOU TO ANOTHER WORLD . . . BEYOND Krishna, Buddha, and Jesus, beyond God consciousness and religions, beyond your discipline in the methods of yoga and transcendental meditation . . . into that emptiness of who you truly are. You are that presence of waves of noumenal energy, the waves which are actualized by the mind through phenomenal attributes. The nature of your reality is not that of a physical being but more of metaphysical being-ness. The idea of 'I', 'me', and 'self' is deceptive for you. It is that state of total awareness, which unfolds in the mind to perceive all that exists in this universe. Meaning, existence appears because you are aware, otherwise it does not.

Sit quietly and watch your mind and enter into your inner self, that ocean of awareness. Simply observe. If it is a thought responding to your consciousness, then it is coming from your mind. However, if you watch your brain without any analytical thinking, you spontaneously enter into that spacious awareness where you perceive in absoluteness without any duality. You enter into that space between you and your thoughts. You go beyond the power of the mind or ego into the domain of the spirit, which has no identification with any 'me or mine'. You snap yourself out of those past and future thoughts and enter into that eternal existential moment of now. You are that supreme potential energy, which has this ability to go beyond the limitations of the mind of just working from the past and the future in order to combine all three—past, present, and future back into its existential now.

You are that cosmic energy minus that 'I', the true self in an 'I-less' state of being-ness, which is responsible for keeping your mind alive, awake, aware, and conscious. You are that impersonal self; watching and witnessing, uninvolved and unaffected over that personal thinking self, encased in a brain that permits you to decipher the difference between a cluttered mind and emptiness.

This true self, the raw cosmic energy is full of nothing; as it is, the way it is endowed with many attributes, the highest of which has been ascribed as that of being aware. It is absolute as one in unity and continuity without any choice or condemnation, rationalization or judgment—just pure potential waves of energy exhibiting its prime attribute of sheer watching and witnessing. Awaken that attribute residing within the superconscious section of your mind, for that is who you are—the supreme energy, which the sages referred to as *Parabrahman*, *Paramatma*—the Cosmic God.

Life travels along with a triangle; the two flat corners are the body and mind triangulating to a point reflecting consciousness. The centre of this triangle is that witness. When you persist as a witness, consciousness becomes free from its dual base of experiencing into this and that, for its likes and dislikes, realizing the true self in purity.

In that emptiness of the superconscious section within the mind, there are waves of pure potential energy dormant and passive. There is neither an attraction nor repulsion, unaffected by anything. However, when the same dormant energy vibrates and collides, there is a particular reverberation, a specific movement from which awareness emerges. Changes occur, and within that space and time, creation materializes until its duration is complete dissipating back into that same quiescence.

Creation, destruction, and recreation take place within the expanse of this infinitude. Awareness brings about an inevitable discovery of what was already there, whenever there is the desire to play in duality for a limited period in space and time and return to its limitless self in that spaceless and timeless realm, we refer to the universe. Allow it to play through your illusory mind—observe, for you are not the mind. You, as a part of that supreme universal spirit, are merely supposed to watch and witness the body and mind playing a dual role in illusions, which we refer to as *Lila* (the divine play).

You are not the thinker, knower, doer, experiencer, or enjoyer. You are simply a permanent part of that observation trapped in mind, for all changes occur just temporarily within that conscious mind to experience the perception of duality called life. You are simply the presence of that aware energy, the witnessing force, entrapped inside an individual brain, which we refer to as the soul—the individual observer. Engage with that intangible observer, watch, and witness, and you will see how the mind plays in illusions, presuming everything to be tangible. It is just a chimaera; do not be fooled by *your* mind or any of its psychic methods. The mind cannot make you spiritual because you are already that—a spiritual presence comprising waves of aware energy going through a human experience playing a role of an observer, which we refer to as the soul.

Reality is one and unchanging, maintaining many attributes or interpretations. It is the total of all that exists—that which is immutable, without any birth or death, meaning, one without a second. And what your mind observes and comprehends are temporary interpretations or mere reflections of the real in myriad manifestations. Illusions are what seems to be real is not without indicating that it is unreal, for all that exists is only one and real. Awareness is the absolute, unchanging reality within which matter and consciousness emerge for that while they exist. They, in turn, continuously change from moment to moment within any space and time. Awareness is the only existent, which neither changes nor becomes anything, always remaining the same.

All changes that you observe take place only in the body and mind or, say, in the field of light that the sun emits, the clouds which disappear in that endless sky, and the waves for those moments arise and subside back in the ocean. You, as a part of that total awareness, remain changeless, eternally as pure awareness, the ultimate ground and substance of everything. You remain passive and dormant, signifying nothing, unless awakened by the mind . . . not as an 'I' but allowing the metaphysical soul to become that watcher of that physical doer, doing what is to be done.

Be who you are, as you are making your mind serene and still. Spirituality is a process of the mind, which you are not; you are that universal spirit enclosed in an individual soul going through a human experience. Spirituality is more of applied psychology rather than being spiritual. I reiterate, you are that spirit, free from all methods, discipline, practices, and concepts provided by the mind in the form of meditation, yoga, vipassana, ta'i chi, etc. You are that being-ness of aware energy. You cannot become that, for you are already that, which *is* always there, and in that is-ness, you remain thoughtless and choiceless.

The becoming is of the mind into this or that for consciousness to experience life like waves that disappear in the ocean and clouds that fade away in the sky, and the sunlight that loses its intensity dissipating into the infinite universe. Likewise, consciousness, too, disperses into that endless expanse of raw cosmic energy along with body and mind after death. Once you come to know and understand the distinction between the non-dual constant awareness and the ever-changing dual consciousness, your mind shall transcend towards that oneness of the ultimate reality.

I repeat, the spirit never demands any effort, change, or activity; it merely watches and witnesses your mind playing games of illusions. You are, as you are, the presence of universal awareness, and you do not change from being that spirit. Your mind is always tied to the past in destiny and karmas; you are not. You, as the spirit are free from every causation. To comprehend this higher knowledge of the self, the mind is supposed to go beyond those ancient scriptures, which administer the mind towards mindfulness. Go beyond the teachings of Buddha, Krishna, and Jesus, and enter into the realm of that actual self where there is total freedom in a new awareness: 'Aham Brahmasmi'—I am that spiritual awareness, conscious energy.

The spirit, I repeat, is not bound to any scriptures, sages, or sensuality, so why impede the mind? Go beyond the cognitive mind and be that witnessing self, where the spirit resides and the mind observes, you will be free from all doership. Be who you are, a witness, a mere onlooker via soul of everything. Even science states that by the very act of observation, the observer affects the observed reality. The body and mind are like waves in an ocean, which come and go. A wave without the sea is nothing; the essence is in the water. Similarly, material consciousness is a wave, while the Brahman/spirit is that ocean of energy, the highest attribute of which is awareness—the essence of everything.

Be alert and keep observing; you shall enter the nature of your true reality. When you watch existentially on the spur of every moment, the mind is still . . . an effortless state of being-ness, choiceless, and thoughtless. You are in that present moment without any past or future thoughts disturbing the now. When the mind becomes quiet and still, desire, feelings, and fear vanish; the observer, observing the observed, becomes one from that intensity of observation, which you are. The moment the mind applies any sort of effort to think and practise, say, methods of meditation or samadhi, there is motivation coming out of some desire to control the mind. On the other hand, continuous observation in spontaneity itself is an effortless meditation; other self-help techniques are just meant to treat and tame the mind.

You are not the mind; it belongs to your observer, the soul. The mind will keep changing, expanding, evolving, and transforming from your thinker, but you are neither that; you are the unchanging part of that universal spirit. When *beyond-ness* awakens, the mind evolves, evolution persists, maturing with time. Materiality flourishes because the mind is designed for that. However, when the mind is still, the spiritual facet awakens, observation alone remains in total awareness. So far as the spirit is concerned, there is no becoming; what exists is only the presence of that being-ness, as it is, the way it is, existentially in its being-ness, in order to activate and make the mind alive.

No doubt, the motivation to transcend your mind through discipline is also necessary because it promotes the mind to a higher level of consciousness with grace and poise. It is required to bring in that harmony, where your body walks on a tightrope, balancing both ends of the pole—the material and the spiritual, the personal and the transpersonal. But unfortunately, due to sheer ignorance, the material overshadows the spiritual, thus, disturbing the whole act of life.

Efforts of any sort are not going to make you spiritual, even though they might bring you closer towards the spirit in higher consciousness. So long as duality persists, the spirit remains aloof from the other two—body and mind. The spirit requires freedom from the mind with its excess baggage of personal identifications and emotional attachments. It does not expect or demand any transcendence from the mind to reveal the truth of who you already are. All that is required is the higher knowledge and understanding of the ultimate reality, which is spaceless, timeless, changeless, limitless, eternal, and the one without a second.

The fundamental characteristic of the mind is to believe, whereas the spirit forever knows. All conflicts arise because of beliefs, continuously differing from one to another. They create bondage with the material or the illusory world. When we believe the body and mind to be factual and everlasting, it becomes the cause for desire and fear, misery and suffering in identification with attachments. We should always keep in mind; the *thinker* is none other than a bundle of thoughts, which you are not.

The spirit knows through its knowing, appreciating the fact that all is one. Based on beliefs, different minds express and project their opinions in different ways. However, that is not true; the truth is one, as it is, the way it is, existential in every moment that it exists, the moment the mind defines truth . . . it is bound to differ. When one has self-knowledge with clarity, the spirit awakens, and the mind becomes one with the Supreme. Hence, the world is full of beliefs, but we, as a part of the universal spirit, are always beyond every conviction and conceptualization, conceived by the mind. Hence, please be very careful about what you believe, follow, or blindly imbibe from here and there.

When you observe from the soul, remaining still by keeping the mind free from thoughts and beliefs, there will be less conflict against any aspect of life—whether it is ego, religion, philosophy, desire, fear, anxiety, or misery. Allow the mind to flow in the direction that it wishes freely. Holistically, you will learn how to accept all attributes, positive or negative, with equal grace, poise, and respect. An alert-observant mind becomes aware and conscious, observes from one moment to the next in every present moment. It attentively and consciously experiences the situation to evolve and transform.

Enlightenment is nothing but a realization of maturing, resulting from experiencing the concerned subject to existentially attain bliss. Therefore, enlightenment is not a moment of eureka, but a realized experience. It is an ongoing experience, which takes place through a disciplined mind, enlightening itself from one beyond into another without any end.

Alternatively, observation is the initial stage in spontaneity, which occurs much before the commencement of any thoughts of doing anything. It is a proactive stage of action in thoughtlessness where the superconscious section of the mind has merely observed without any analysis, evaluation, or choice. This primordial observation is genuine and unbiased, and it will not make your mind do anything wrong. It is proactive in its action and not emotionally or desirously reactive. At this point, the mind is untainted, without thinking in self-interest and has become aware and conscious through sheer observation.

The spontaneous awareness emerging through such observation generally extends into the next stage. Thoughts of materiality arise out of self-consciousness, the mind chooses in duality with relativity; memory and intellect determine, experience, and infer to realize material living. Thus, materiality occurs only after the mind separates the oneness of this immediate non-dual energy in its duality of this or that, for its likes and dislikes due to which we enter into a reactive cycle of pleasure and pain.

It is this initial spontaneous moment of observation that is non-dual and complete in its wholesomeness. The moment the cognitive mind starts to think, the brain's activity commences and desires to emerge. The conscious and the subconscious element responsible for separating every sensation to choose between this and that begins. Therefore, irrespective of whether the mind is dreaming, thinking, or doing—for a spiritual person—it is all the same. Moreover, in the East, if the mind is functioning unconsciously from a subconscious state of mind, which is generally the case, it is considered to be asleep.

A material mind is designed to work subconsciously, not demanding any conscious or creative inputs. When the mind is conscious, it slows the speed of thinking. It excessively functions unconsciously, meaning, randomly and recklessly—multitasking from the subconscious section from its memory and intellect. A subconscious mind *reacting* under emotional desires—when physically awake—determines, experiences, and realizes mostly on what it believes from its past knowledge of all that it does. It forms the sum or aggregate of a material doership.

However, if and when the mind spontaneously or proactively experiences the doings of the mind without the aid of a constant stream of subconscious thoughts, it is considered to be creative as well as spiritual, otherwise, it could be reactive. It infuses fresh energy effortlessly into what it proactively experiences. Therefore, it is essential to note here that the mind, which is proactive, still, and present from one moment to the next, existentially performs in mindfulness with higher intelligence and creativity, which we refer to as meditative awareness or mindfulness.

Secondly, a spiritual person is dispassionate about every feeling of the mind. He or she neither accepts nor rejects and is sensitive to everything that is around. Meaning, the individual is neither sentimental nor emotional to any aspect of life. He or she is free and non-attached to the personal and desirous thoughts prevailing in the mind. He or she is a witness or an onlooker to his self-consciousness to whatever the mind refers, relates, or reflects and is, thus, free from all its bindings in beliefs. He does not identify with any name, gender, religion, caste, or community, for he is none other than the presence of observation seated within the mind. He knows that he is just that witnessing self with the sole purpose of making the mind aware and conscious to experience a life of dualities with relativity and rationally. Unaffected and uninvolved, remaining as a witness, he is neither attracted nor repulsed towards anything to which the mind identifies or attaches.

Only when you liberate your thinking self from worldly passions and mental compassions, your impersonal self awakens in the impartial presence of your being-ness. The mind becomes alert and aware of all that is around. There are no ideas, desires, feelings, or sensations of any emotional thoughts to disturb the purity of your observation. You become free from all bindings. You are not that thinking self, emerging from the body and mind. You are a witness to this universe, observing through the spiritual presence—beyond dharma and karma. When you understand the essence and the difference between the higher knowledge (*Para Vidya*) and the lower knowledge (*Apara*)—spiritual and the material—the mind becomes capable of balancing the two to live a life of fulfilment in its wholesomeness.

Know and understand the spirit to celebrate life. You are not that seeker, seeking the sought; observer, observing the observed; or even that doer, doing the done. That is all for your mind to perform. You are simply that observation in the form of awareness, which is independent and not supported by body, mind, or even consciousness. Unless your consciousness is pure and total, liberation will always back away, and the soul will remain bound to attachments. Therefore, you are merely that presence of awareness embodied in an individual body, mind, and soul of a transitory *self in mid-reality,* which is only an illusion—a mere reflection of your *ultimate reality.*

If you wish to taste eternal, awareness is that force . . . the core from which the field of intelligence manifests in the form of consciousness. When the light of awareness focuses on objects without identifying or attaching emotionally through desires, you merely witness them. The world is there for your consciousness to experience and will be there even after it disappears after death. For it is not your consciousness that sees everything, it is the core energy of awareness that makes it possible. The basis of all—the force behind all consciousness—is nothing but aware energy. Awareness is there in the presence and in the absence of consciousness, too, for everything, including the universe, exists solely because we are aware. Our ultimate self, please keep in mind, resides in the present moment, fully aware without any thoughts.

Chapter 3

LETTING GO OF SPIRITUALITY

'One of the most bizarre premises of quantum theory, which has long fascinated philosophers and physicists alike, states that by the very act of watching, the observer affects the observed reality.'

—Weizmann Institute of Science

THERE IS NO COMMON MEANING OF SPIRITUALITY; THE subject has developed over time and can accommodate many perspectives. It often relates to the meaning and purpose of life, determining who we are and what is the true nature of our reality. The definition has broadened from traditional religious processes to include many mental qualities of life. My attempts on the spiritual power series have primarily centred on spiritual awareness, which embraces the idea of an *ultimate, intangible, aware reality*. I have mostly expressed the discipline of religion aiming to present Advaita Vedanta with a scientific approach based on Hindu universalism. The reason, Hinduism is basically not a religion but a way of life towards eternities; how to awaken and liberate your spirit from mental identifications and attachments towards that non-dual path in search of peace and tranquillity.

Hinduism and the subject of spiritualism are synonymous since both equate the self as 'brahman/energy', which is responsible to make the mind aware and conscious of what it experiences considering the same to be the highest attribute of the absolute cosmic raw energy. The purpose of writing this volume is to expound on the spirit, which is generally ignored in the triad of our body-mind and soul, so that we may understand all three as one in totality. Meaning, to be spiritual is to discover that ultimate truth equating and establishing the relationship between the transpersonal with the personal. The spirit transcends beyond individual identifications and attachments to encompass a wider perspective of all three— body, mind, and the soul—as one.

In this chapter, we shall dwell more on this truth. I am the presence of the spirit of awareness; my nature is that of aware conscious energy, which oversees my mind and its body. Scientifically, the body is gross condensed energy, and the mind is that subtle operating system embodied in a physical brain subconsciously functioning under duality in an unconscious manner. However, we also consist of the spirit contained in a soul comprising non-dual waves of energy in the form of awareness. It is that being-ness, which incorporates the core essence of our reality unfolding for the mind all that it knows, from the subatomic to the stars.

My emphasis here is based entirely on this abstract nature of reality, which is generally overlooked or ignored by many because of its complex nature. Hindu scriptures describe two categories of knowledge—the lower knowledge is to understand and experience the phenomenal world within the ambit of the human self and the human gods and a higher knowledge is meant for an understanding of the noumenal spirit as the 'supreme self'.

The subject of spiritualism is more of understanding the difference between the being and the non-being. By way of writing or speaking, it may sound simple, but to explore and discover the complex nature of this intrinsic non-being self provides the inherent essence and substance of our true nature of reality. Those who confine themselves thinking only of body and mind become susceptible to the ego, leading to conflicts and grief. Therefore, the mind on a physical level remains separated and limited from the whole, suffering from mess to misery, unless the spirit within awakens to enlighten the mind—*who, what, and how we are.*

Essentially, from the spiritual prospect, I am that absolute whole, the illumined self, like the sun—a force of aware energy emitting its field of light in the form of knowledge (consciousness). No guru, book, or ashram can help identify *who you are.* The only way is to *observe, witness, understand, and know thyself.* Therefore, rather than running here and there, blindly following some guru or another, let us try to discover that truth, the divine within, and exercise how to live in that spiritual oneness with humanity in humility.

Allow me to take you on such a path and show you how to walk along with it psychologically. Though I do not have the authority to claim there is anything wrong with our world; certainly, there seems to be some confusion of how we interact with this world. It appears to be grossly imbalanced between the colossal progress made by technology and digitalization compared to the inner peace and joy we so desperately seek. Science has provided us with ample comforts but not given enough credence to know and understand the true nature of our inner reality.

Most scientists, psychiatrists, and psychologists have viewed the nature of our reality in a skewed manner—the reason for widespread despair and depression. What we see today is a mad, mad world that is falling apart mentally, socially, morally, emotionally, and environmentally and is always under fear and insecurity, which, in turn, makes us live a false life full of blind beliefs into this or that.

For thousands of years, our minds have been prejudiced and conditioned by science, religion, and spirituality, imposing multitude ways and means of how to transcend, transform, and transfigure our 'me and mine' into a profound human being. This transformation yet remains a distant dream. We are simply not calm, content, and counterpoised between the material and the spiritual. We continue to seek religious and spiritual formulae to make our minds still, serene, and stable so that we may be proud of our individuality. But, how many of us can truthfully claim to have realized a wholesome way of living? All we have achieved is to convert more people from one religion into another to fight and kill one another.

It is evident that our spiritual celebrities, through their institutions, have become billionaires from their profound preaching. But what about us mortals? Even after listening to all their sermons, we remain in the same level of ego-consciousness, concerned only about our 'me and mine', destroying and consuming our Mother Nature irresponsibly. Look around, within and out, you will not find any fulfilment despite possessing enough health, wealth, and knowledge. Most of us talk of high ideals but do not walk that path. The reason, what we have is a wavering unconscious mind running amok subconsciously. We have simply deviated from our actual self to a presumed personality. All this has happened despite knowing we are the most superior living creatures on this earth and have not behaved in the manner that we should; our material values have replaced devotion and selflessness.

Spiritualism bestows upon us the higher knowledge of the impersonal, impartial, formless spirit, which requires no effort or practice from the mind. Whereas, the course of spirituality imparts psychic efforts and methods on how to discipline and elevate the consciousness of our mind, from the lower self (ego) towards that higher self in divinity. However, despite all these mental exercises, like meditation and yoga, the brain bounces back with extra vigour to its original ego-self.

Advaita Vedanta has categorically rejected the concept of dualism, denying the role of the senses and the intellect for any spiritual upliftment. So long as the mind differentiates between oneself and another, that feeling of survival of the fittest arises, separating everything into this or that leading towards ego and conflicts. It has strongly prophesied: All that exists is the spirit of awareness in unity and continuity, the presence of formless waves of aware energy, the substratum of everything from which everything appears and disappears. All transitory forms of life, including what you see in the universe, are mere appearances superimposed on the presence of this highest attribute of raw cosmic energy we refer to as awareness. There is no second existence because all objects present in the universe eventually disappear into that absolute dark energy after the culmination of their purpose.

Pleasure and pain are states of the mind and it is only when we identify them as 'me and mine' and link them to our physical identity that the soul becomes bound and imprisoned in its mind. A human mind is essentially designed to process past thoughts and project them into the future without paying any attention to the present. However, when the mind comes to know it is being watched, it behaves itself. In such a state, the mind effortlessly stops thinking and becomes aware and conscious of the present moment and is better equipped to handle any situation in an appropriate manner. This means, the moment you—the presence of that spirit—watch and witness the mind, it becomes shy, aware, and conscious and starts to behave appropriately, knowing that some source is watching over its actions.

Therefore, instead of trying to control or suppress thought processes with breathing exercises or any psychic effort, we should first explore the nature of our actual reality—what is this spirit that we keep speaking about? What does it mean to be spiritual? It becomes far more comfortable to balance the personal with that impersonal self once you understand the subject of spiritualism from its fundamental essence. This is where the matter of the spirit supersedes from its practices of spirituality simply because it is that inner transcendent residing within, which does not require any effort from your mind. You can never reach the spirit through your mind; you will need to go beyond into that soul to apprehend your spiritual self.

Spiritualism tells us you are already the potential presence of a certain quotient of that universal spirit—enlightened in all respects. Practising methods of spirituality will only make your mind stronger, making it more receptive to accept this core ingredient, your being-ness as the spirit. Spirituality is more of a reformative process of becoming-ness needed for the cognitive mind to elevate its consciousness through the transitory physical being. It will only take you towards the periphery of the centre. The core is that impersonal spirit, the abstract spiritual self, which is imperative for you to know and clearly understand in order to not engage and control but *awaken* that centre.

After practising various methods of spirituality conceptualised by the mind, the ego-consciousness temporarily comes closer to the nature of your actual reality, the spirit. These methods do not last for long, simply because the mind is uncontrollable. If you notice, it bounces back with extra vigour to its original self. Since you are already a spiritual being going through a human experience, you are not required to do anything to become spiritual. In order to be who you are, you simply need to ask your mind how to awaken that spirit.

In actuality, we are fundamentally the presence of waves of absolute aware energy/spirit, not as a being but in that being-ness perceiving all that exists via consciousness. You already are that potential divine spirit—Aham Brahmasmi or *Shivohum*[1]. All you need is an alert, attentive mind to witness and awaken that dormant spirit residing within to make the mind, first, aware and, then, conscious of what it perceives and experiences. In short, *awareness is the essence of perception and consciousness is the essence of experiencing*. Both conjoin as a unitary factor in a force-field relationship.

So, how does one go beyond the processes of spirituality and awaken this spirit? As mentioned above, the practice of spirituality is a reformative process of the mind that requires motivation (desire) and effort to undertake any exercise.

And every step, in one way or another, enhances the factor of 'me' in the body and mind, supporting and nourishing that thinking 'I' in a false superiority. Your mind believes it has done something transcendental. Always remember, the ego-mind is that doer, doing through the mind all that needs to be done. The soul, meaning, the witnessing self, is that observer that only observes through its force of energy, the spirit residing within and does nothing more. Any motivation for the practices of spirituality originates solely from the same ego-mind, for the mind, and by the mind. In no way does it awaken the dormant spirit contained in an individual soul. If any motivation is to discipline, relax, and transcend the mind, it cannot be spiritual. Thus, every practice creates an experience, which itself is the function of the mind to elevate its consciousness.

The soul, which contains the universal spirit, is already that divine and does not require any experiencing. It is that eternal incarnate, which does not require any reincarnation. It is independent of the cognitive or sensory mind and, hence, does not require any practising or mental exercises. To be spiritual, all that your mind needs is to be alert and attentive; it needs to self-observe from the soul to awaken itself so that your mind becomes aware and conscious and does not function blindly from its subconscious section. Only after the brain is fully alert and attentive, you, as the spirit, via the soul will be able to observe the devious ways of that thinking mind. It is this self-knowledge that provides the understanding as to why you should continuously and truthfully watch and witness your inner self without any prejudices or justifications.

The effort applied for practising meditation and yoga will benefit you therapeutically for the sake of your body and mind but not for the spirit. The spirit is already enlightened; it merely needs awakening through inner observation. True meditation is but an *effortless* and silent movement of aware energy, which occurs and concurs in the present moment, if and when your mind is alert and thoughtlessly attentive to activate itself to become spontaneously aware. Therefore, you need not make any effort to practise meditation unless it is therapeutically required to relax a disturbed body and mind for a short while.

The spirit is that being-ness, the presence of that inner awareness, and it merely requires freedom from the cognitive mind. The moment the mind becomes motivated and makes efforts to practise, you—the spirit—become bound and are not free. However, for the spirit to be free, you need not *become* aware of the sake of making your mind aware, for you are already that awareness. Thus, the presence of awareness (understanding) is the awareness of that presence, which is considered to be the self-knowledge. The intensity of your mental awareness needs to *reflect* effortlessly through your consciousness for others to see how spiritual you are.

The spirit is that absolute aware energy, which manifests in mind as the witnessing awareness. This ingredient materialises on its own in sheer observation and nothing else. The rest happens effortlessly. In its primordial state, while observing, awareness is spontaneous, thoughtless, and choiceless, signifying the subjective reality of who you are. Pure observation reveals what is being observed, as it is in the present moment through its consciousness of what you are watching . . . in its valid and actual observation.

After that, it extends in the zone of the analytical thinking mind, which takes over to make your body feel, think, imagine, believe, fantasise, analyze, and choose in duality with relativity, making efforts to experience, infer, and realize all that is being observed. Hence, the spirit solely conducts itself initially during the presence of observation to make your mind aware and conscious of what it perceives. It is primordial and occurs in the present moment with zero past or future thoughts.

Mind, on the other hand, is that operating system to work for your *thinking self* in self-interest. Meaning, it gets activated only after the mind becomes aware and conscious of functioning in duality, consciously or subconsciously, in order to choose between any two related factors for it to experience and realize. Life commonly is nothing but a series of such experiences in cumulative thoughts to establish its identifications in emotional attachments—a state of its individuality or consciousness, taking you on a roller-coaster ride, either towards divinity or that devil.

Therefore, the thinking mind is that doer and enjoyer, doing to claim something for its selfish interest, the trophy for what it has done. All thoughts originate from the past— the memory—which further gets analyzed via the intellect. It is meant to determine, experience, and infer. Memory is that centre, which is also responsible for reminding you of your personal or physical name, gender, and identity projecting your personal 'I'. All these inputs are derived from the cognitive mind, which is not the actual 'you'. Since that selfish, separated *thinker* is nothing but a bundle of personal and biased thoughts. The essential 'you' is not a being or a person but waves of constant-flowing 'I-less' state of being-ness in the eternal now, which is impersonal and unbiased.

I reiterate, the thinker or that 'doer' is none other than the ego or self-consciousness, which wrongly presumes its transitory nature to be the true self, which it is not. This sort of self is created out of a culmination of tightly held emotional thoughts originating from the memory, which is concerned primarily for its identity, accumulations, and attachments. If you simply observe your thoughts, where they come from and where they go, the mind discovers this sense of self is merely an illusion. Thus, the person you think yourself to be is just another *belief* and does not genuinely exist.

The spirit is the presence of that transpersonal universal 'I', which has no individual identity, for that would be separating the unity of one into two. I repeat for the sake of clarification: The thinker, ego-self, or that doer is none other than the culmination of thoughts emerging to become an experiencer while it exists. For example, in a moving vehicle, the spirit is that drive (subject) and the brain is that driver, driving (through the mind) the driven (the object). The individually embedded spirit present within an individual mind, the section we refer to as the soul, is also called as the witnessing self. It is called a *self*, despite being present as waves of aware energy, only because these waves have been entrapped in an individual capacity within any body and mind, which we also, at times, refer to as the 'witnessing or pure consciousness'.

An unconscious body and mind, because of all its subconscious doing, has this illusory feeling of being eternal, which it is not. The individual spirit, in our case, is that presence of total awareness in the superconscious section of the mind—the observatory power that silently witnesses all that the mind does. Hence, do not mix the two. The spirit is that *force* or authority of the divine and consciousness is its *field* of illumination. The mind is that necessary software wherein consciousness experiences, expands, and evolves in order to transcend and transform towards its realization of absoluteness from where it separated.

The spirit residing within your mind only needs to be awakened to observe all that the mind continuously does. Thus, always remember, since the soul is individualized, it is that *observer* and your mind is the experiencer. However, the actual 'you' as the universal spirit is sheer *observation*, the presence of the ultimate cosmic waves of absolute aware energy entrapped in a human mind.

Spirituality, in actuality, refers to that mental process of reformation, which attempts to take your mind towards the presence of your true nature in absoluteness. However, the authentic role of the spirit, the subject of 'who you are' representing itself as a witness being complex has been avoided and is not well elaborated by our masters. Majority of the gurus, while explaining to the masses, prefer mixing this philosophical context with mythical and mystical religious connotations since it becomes simpler with magical fables, rituals, and dogmas. Masters of this subject seldom stress upon the fact that a witness/observer influences the mind and affects the observed reality. This, however, has been well explained and elaborated by science in 'The Observer Effect'[2].

To be spiritual, you just need to *flow, observe, and surf* between the material and the spiritual with your third eye open. It is only during these spontaneous moments of sheer observation that the mind becomes proactive and non-dual in totality (spiritual). Later, when the mind extends into thoughts, the process of duality commences (material). Thoughts are required to relate one dual factor to another for the mind to choose between this and that to experience consciously or, otherwise, according to its likes and dislikes.

All complex principles and formulae like '*turiya*' (pure consciousness) to '*turiyatita*' (to become Shiva) are fantasies of the mind to realize that eternal self. You are already that potential *Shivohum*—the potential divine—and all that is required is to awaken that 'third eye'. Being absolute in the form of spirit is an independent state of the non-physical, a condition of being formless, which the dependent state of body and brain are not. Hence, a mind can never realize this state of oneness while you are physically alive. What is required is for all three—body-mind and the soul—to lucidly interact and understand each other, in totality and unity, as one. The thinking self needs to utilise this potential divine balancing the material mind with the inner spiritual insight in a calm, content, and moderate manner.

If you wish to go beyond and become celestial, supernal, or saintly—in a state of what is called *ananda myoksha*—you need to practise and make efforts to be selfless, fearless, and dispassionate. It is meant for very few who are ready to sacrifice their personal lives, like Mahatma Gandhi, to experience and realize. With the above three qualities, he was able to defeat the British without firing a single bullet.

Our third factor, the soul/spirit, is generally ignored with most of us not being aware or being confused about its presence. Hence, when the mind is doing something, it remains selfish, and the spirit remains dormant. Thinking, reacting, and experiencing anything *personally* refers to materiality, whereas proacting selflessly and fearlessly with alert observation—*effortlessly and dispassionately in an impersonal manner* from the non-dual section of the mind— is considered to be spiritual.

* * *

There is utter confusion today about the subject of spiritualism. It differs in its understanding from the East to the West, and from one religion to another based on beliefs turning into faith. The mind too overly exerts and expresses from the personal thinking state, refusing to familiarize and accept the nature of its actual reality in that of a formless, impersonal state. When one lives under illusions of its true self, you can imagine the doubt, disorder, and fear it creates.

The illusory mind has given some eminent neuroscientists enough valid reasons to declare that a human mind excessively functions from its subconscious section unconsciously. We blindly follow the tenets and methods of yoga, zen, vipassana, samadhi, meditation, etc., desiring some spiritual results out of them for our future, wrongly presuming we have become spiritual. We believe in fantasies of reincarnation, past life regression, and rebirth thinking we are spiritual. We mistakenly consider religion, which separates one from another, to be spiritual reformation. Most beliefs, I would say, are illusions; they have no verifiable evidence since they differ from one another, leading to conflicts and misunderstanding about the true nature of our reality.

We are living in illusions of this and that, considering and concluding the mind as the eternal thinker. We have drifted further away from being spiritual. There is no proper balance between the two selves—the material and the spiritual. We are gradually becoming worse, self-obsessed, and selfish. All this is evident when we observe the manner our collective minds are behaving in the modern era. All psychic methods of spirituality have led us into a bigger doubt. What we have gained is more of desire, insecurity, and fear, simply because we have not been able to distinguish between the spirit and the mind. Even after gaining some knowledge of spirituality and practising to discipline the mind, the desirous psychological self—the ego—exists, sustains, and sways our life.

We remain silent or ignorant of our permanent universal presence, which speaks only of oneness in unity and continuity. We remain egoist with our illusory identity of 'me and mine' revolving and clinging to likes and dislikes. Our minds are unable to see any fundamental change besides what it projects to others. The mind has a habit of bouncing back, separating one from another; it is fundamentally designed to be selfish and live under fear for its self-preservation.

I reiterate, the spirit requires your mind only to be alert, attentive, and truthful to observe non-selectively. At that moment, your mind, before any thoughts, is in the present moment and is silent from any chatter. The moment you apply any effort, it will be from the mind and not the spirit. The cause of any conflict or misery arises because we were never told, nor were we prepared to *observe our inner thoughts truthfully* from the angle of the spirit and not the mind. We should keep in mind that spirituality is an experiential journey to transcend the mind into higher consciousness. However, we should also know that experiencing itself is an operating field originating from the cognitive mind. The spirit does not require any experiencing to transcend anywhere. It is already that *transcendent* residing within, which we need to understand with clarity and not practice. Always remember, you—as the soul—is the observer and mind is that experiencer.

Your mind returns from all those efforts, methods, and techniques to the same point where it started. Intelligent 'masters' can easily fool the masses claiming they have abolished their false ego-self, which is sheer rubbish. The mind is ego and ego is the mind. You can spend as much money, time, and effort proving to others how great these practices are, but they will only lead to a better disciplining of the mind. Deep down, if you are true to your thinking self, you will know your mind is that same egoist self, trying to become that something, which you are not. Inwardly you know, and those who also observe very well know, that your thinking self survives in ego. We continue to function subconsciously in an unconscious manner, thriving on desire, identifications, and attachments, trying to project our superiority over the other.

The fundamental understanding of the nature of your reality has been biased right from the beginning. You have been severely conditioned that these few lines attempting to reveal the truth may not convince you. However, at least, it will make you think, and that may herald a new beginning. It may help you understand that all you require from any master is only to point towards the right direction in which to traverse. If this indication is faulty, the results, too, are bound to be, facilitating mess to misery, which is evident today. Each one is trying to snatch from the environment, more than he or she can consume.

For consciousness to transcend, the mind requires the spirit or that observing self to make your mind aware and conscious. For that, you need to be more of a keen observer rather than an experiencer. To be spiritual, you do not need the cognitive self, but the mind minus the thoughts. The spirit does not require any mental beliefs or methods. What mind generally lacks is that habit to keenly and consistently witness its thinking self. For that, you need to be existentially alert and attentive to make your mind aware and conscious from one moment to the next. Effortlessly, without thinking, you will proactively discard what is not favourable and undertake your tasks spontaneously with least resistance.

Hence, since both the mind and the spirit are distinct, you require a different approach for both; otherwise, there is confusion, and you remain under a false persona. Both require their independent attention, the mind with spirituality (meditative processes of yoga) and the spirit through constant, truthful, and alert observation from your super consciousness.

The spirit is entrapped in your mind. It has been separated and fragmented into your subconscious and conscious sections. It wishes to be free to flow and witness the material as well as the spiritual. I repeat, it does not require any psychic transcendence because it is already that potential transcendent—Tat Tvam Asi or Thou Art That. Your ego in ignorance is directly attaching another medal: 'I have become spiritual because I meditate and do yoga.' Sorry, it is not your spirit but only your mind that requires that discipline!

Therefore, spirituality is purely a mental process to transcend and discipline your mind from one level to another. All it does is make your brain better, more humane, and a little more caring, presuming that other circumstances do not hinder your state of mental discipline. However, as long as the mind is there, the ego is present; both are equally required—material for that physical progress and comforts and the spiritual to surrender the mind with selflessness and humility for the sake of oneness of who and what you are in the ultimate reality. Hereafter, we enter deep into the subject of spiritualism, for this whole volume has been dedicated to simplify and clarify the dictum behind 'Thou Art That'.

Chapter 4

AWARENESS AND CONSCIOUSNESS

'Meditate on yourself as motionless awareness,
free from any dualism, giving up the mistaken
idea that you are just a derivative consciousness
or anything external or internal.'

—John Richards, Ashtavakra Gita (1.13)

AWARENESS AND CONSCIOUSNESS CONSTITUTE THE former being the subject and the latter its object, the context, and its content. Meaning, awareness is that quality and consciousness is its quantum. Both have a force-field relationship and are the *essence* of perception of all living creatures. They are responsible for creating all the concepts devised by the mind to decipher and determine, through evolution, the tangible and the intangible in totality—the whole universe. Awareness is that *sole unchanging existence,* which is primordial and eternal and is the highest attribute of energy, which precedes all that we perceive and conceive. It is that transcendental state of non-duality. The rest, meaning, whatever we see and observe in the entire universe unfolds all because of awareness, for they exist in order to introduce, over time, one concept after another.

In science, quantum field theory may be close to discovering the true nature of *what is real* in our subatomic world. Yet, differences of opinion amongst scientists remain with regards to energy simultaneously behaving as a wave as well as a particle in duality. When an observer is watching, quantum mechanics states that particles can also behave as waves. In other words, under observation, electrons are compelled to behave like particles and not like waves. Hence, the mere act of observation affects the experimental findings. The question arises, to whom, then, is matter appearing as solid, when it is not? It presupposes a subject, which is, in this case, beyond everything that we perceive—the spirit of awareness as the highest attribute of energy, the one and only reality.

Spiritualism in Hindu scriptures elaborate further: 'Reality is one without a second, changeless, spaceless, timeless, and limitless.' That which changes cannot be real; reality is absolute, non-dual, and independent, not requiring any support. Meaning, there cannot be two realities at any one moment. One is real and the other, whatever we observe and perceive, is an illusion. Therefore, the conclusion is what actually exists is only the highest attribute of energy, which is *awareness*, the substratum of all that exists; the rest are mere temporary forms of waves and particles of energy superimposed on the real by our consciousness. In contrast, they appear in space, time, and causation.

Therefore, the source or the determinant factor with regards to the ultimate knowledge is awareness. It allows the mind to be conscious of what it observes. I repeat, all objects in the universe exist merely because of this highest attribute of energy manifesting as absolute awareness in mind, which—after extending into thoughts—become conscious to experience and infer upon the same, consciously or unconsciously. We need to understand the actual nature of our ultimate reality, one without a second, which never dies. It is that 'I-less' state of being-ness residing within the human mind, which we refer to as awareness.

Now, let us explore what consciousness is all about? It is that state of being aware and responsive to what the mind feels. It is that centralized thought of *what we are* without which we have no other way of knowing that we exist. In fine, it is my wakefulness, which culminates into my individuality. The moment I wake up, I am already aware, and after that, I become conscious of who, what, and where I am. From the subatomic to the stars, probability waves of energy are vibrating and reverberating all around the universe. These waves remain intangible unless we observe them through our eyes as particles of light energy popping in and out of existence. They ripple and reverberate like waves of water in a pond. From amoeba, algae, apes to humans, all have gone through billions of years of evolution.

These possible waves of energy collapsing into particles, according to spiritualism, seem to possess a fundamental characteristic of being aware, for they undergo a sea change of evolving and transforming through an evolution as we see them today.

Therefore, I repeat, the intensity (-ness) of aware energy, signifying as awareness is the cause and the substance for this metamorphosis, and this spiritual feature of energy being aware has been ascribed as the highest attribute of the all-encompassing energy of the universe. Aware energy enables and unfolds to observe, measure, and determine all that we know of the universe.

Consciousness, on the other hand, is the greatest mystery of human life. Science is confused when it comes to an understanding of our abstract conscious entity. It agrees but does not seem to know how this conscious principle awakens the brain-body connection. There is no uniformity even today among philosophers and scientists on the nature of our true reality—whether it is awareness or in the form of our consciousness. Also, whether it is a construct of the mind or paranormal and supernatural. From belief to faith, the confusion continues, and verifiable evidence is yet to materialize. Unfortunately, instead of probing the *potential force* of aware energy, science is more concerned with its resultant field of consciousness.

This confusion probably arose from varied interpretations of our ancient philosophical scriptures, considering the soul to be the eternal and final attribute of energy in the form of universal consciousness. Meaning, presuming its continuity or eternity from one life into another remains a mystery, a matter of blind faith. However, one thing is sure, if subatomic waves and particles can become aware and consequently conscious, we can safely presume that the intensity of individual consciousness exists while we are awake and alive.

There are three aspects we need to keep in mind when we discuss consciousness. First, it is local to the object; meaning, it requires an object to be conscious about and needs to attach to one out of the dual factors that occur in mind as well. Only after that the mind rationalizes and chooses one out of the two for its likes and dislikes. Second, it is entirely dependent upon awareness. You can be conscious of something only after you are aware of the same. Third, it expresses itself in the present moment.

The subject of spiritualism fundamentally relates to two specific words, which are independent yet closely associated as one—awareness and consciousness. Like the sun and the light or the ocean and its waves are associated as one in a force-field relationship, but the former in both examples is independent and the latter is dependent. They may be synonymous with each other, and even if we assume everything, after all, is a bunch of quantum waves, they do differ in their constitution and performance. A seeker surely needs to understand the difference between the two, that is, if one wishes to apprehend the subject of life correctly.

Spiritual awareness is that untainted non-dual energy, which makes the mind spontaneously aware to kick-start its aliveness. It is that immediate knowledge of any situation or fact. It is that force of energy, which radiates its field of illumination in the form of consciousness. Awareness prevails before the 'I am' appears and sustains and after consciousness disappears. Awareness is without consciousness, but consciousness consists only of awareness. Meaning, only after the mind is aware, it becomes conscious, but not otherwise. Consciousness symbolizes the limited body-mind self, whereas awareness is that absolute non-dual energy—the spirit—which permits the soul to play its role in making the mind aware. Thus, awareness is that *force* that radiates through its field of consciousness. All that we perceive exists only because we are aware, and without awareness we can't become conscious of all that exists in this universe.

Consciousness is being aware of and responding to one's surroundings. It constitutes everything that we perceive and experience, providing meaning to our life of all that exists. It is the after-effect of awareness, making the mind conscious, and it is dual by nature. It needs to attach to something for the mind to be mindful. Consciousness is a mental process of experiencing life, whereas spiritual awareness is that spontaneous and choiceless presence of aware energy in any individual occurring with or without any thoughts.

Hence, consciousness is not an ingredient or a thing as it is made out to be, which supposedly travels from one life into another. It is that content or the total of your conscious and subconscious experiencing while you exist, settled in the memory. It forms your unique individuality from all that you experience in life. Consciousness is a construct of the mind, whereas awareness is not. Both awareness and consciousness combine to create your observable (through awareness) and comprehensible (through consciousness) reality as real.

Every form of energy has a potent force with a respective kinetic field. With regards to our subject, energy on visual stimulation in higher frequencies creates visual awareness, which, after obtaining information, radiates a field that communicates in synchrony throughout the brain's network of neural pathways. It is this *force* of aware energy, which radiates a *field* of consciousness—lowest, say, in the case of a rock and highest in the case of a human mind. Therefore, awareness is that ultimate primordial constituent of everything because being absolute is ascribed as the one and the only unchanging, permanent existent—that which is really real.

Consciousness, on the other hand, dissipates with the death of an object. However, the presence of awareness within the brain, the absolute non-dual ingredient, progresses better amongst those living creatures well adapted to the environment towards a gradual evolution along with the cellular progression. The force of awareness retains its identity like the eternal sky. Still, consciousness is like those clouds that appear and disappear, losing their quality and consequently dispersing in the infinite space of the universe. The essential difference between awareness and consciousness is that the former is the force of energy, like the sun, and the latter is its field of radiance, the sunshine that it emits. Both are inherent and intrinsic to each other, like the sun and its rays of light or, say, also like the manner sparks emerge from the flames of any inflammable source.

When the mind initially becomes aware, it is thoughtless and spontaneous; it proactively starts to experience without any thinking. However, when awareness enters further in the brain, a particular field of operation is created, and a certain aware feeling arises—thinking begins, a thinker emerges, and the mind becomes objectively conscious or subconscious (not fully aware) of what it chooses, experiences, infers, and realizes.

Primordial awareness is the original state of the aware spirit. The moment the brain takes over, it splits the same energy into two, relating in duality to discriminate and infer with opposites, consciously or otherwise. However, awareness and consciousness both relate to each other as one, like any flame of fire and the spark it emits. The potential force retains its identity, but the field it radiates has a particular qualitative limitation as it spreads. Like the sun remains potential as the force. But, its field of light energy reduces in quality as it extends into the infinite dark energy, only to dissipate and disappear in the infinitude of our universe. Even though they are intrinsic to each other as one, once the force releases its field of power—say, light energy—it can never return to its source of potential energy. The same has been well explained in the second law of thermodynamics in physics.

Let us go through this thesis again for better clarification. Consciousness operates in a state of duality and depends on a subject-object relationship. It needs to attach to something, to any single relative factor, to be conscious. However, without awareness, there can be no consciousness. Aware energy is that link between the subject and the object. It is that transcendent state of non-duality, which we refer to as the spirit. It is there both before and after consciousness appears and disappears, meaning, before birth and after death.

The highest attribute of energy, the spirit, has been accredited to be that awakened awareness (*Chaitanya*) referred to as Parabrahman or supreme power. It is also called the Paramatma, the abstract, formless God or supreme energy, the eternal, ultimate reality comprising the universe, which only the Hindus relate to. After the universal *spirit* manifests in an individual mind, it goes one stage lower and enters into a subject-object relationship. It is then ascribed as the individual *soul* responsible for making the mind aware and conscious to experience life. The individual soul is a notch less than the spirit, though being in total awareness it is now attributed as the *Antaratma*. It becomes the sole benefactor to develop and evolve the knowledge stored in the memory and the intellect within the mind. And it further reduces in its degree, which we refer to as *Jivatma* in the capacity of ego or self-consciousness.

* * *

Let us now probe how the mind becomes aware.

The *awakening* of the soul takes place if the mind is *alert*. When an alert mind initiates the action of observance, the soul becomes the observer—observing through the mind, making it aware of the object being observed and, after that, if the mind is attentive, conscious. Therefore, whichever direction the mind is alert and attentive, the universal energy responds in the same frequency, and the aware energy manifests and materializes. The degree of its attentiveness determines the level of self-consciousness.

The mind is primarily designed to function on its own, in autopilot, from its memory and intellect. However, energy has this tendency to flow in entropy, so awareness is required to check this disorderly flow of thoughts through its self-consciousness. Commonly, the psychic flow bypasses alert-aware-conscious energy. As a result, the subconscious mind takes over and excessively rules, randomly and recklessly, into this or that from its past awareness. . . . multitasking in an erratic manner, unless it is checked and countered by the conscious section. In due course, the culmination of all experiences—subconscious and the conscious—sum up to form an individual self-consciousness.

The raw universal energy consisting of total awareness (spirit) is the source of core intelligence from which the mind discovers and perceives everything. The energy on its own is never aware of itself but can make the mind aware. It remains passive and materializes as a *witness* after manifesting in the brain. Whenever the mind is alert and observant, the witness-er (soul—a grade less than the entrapped universal spirit) makes the mind aware and conscious. It is that connection between the total universal awareness and the potential human soul—the personal and the transpersonal.

However, the soul may be the last indicator towards the cosmic energy. Still, after the death of the body and mind, both the witness and the witness-er have to contract, dissolve, and vaporize into that raw cosmic energy from where they had originated. You, again, become one with the universe from where you parted. Since you are not that witness but the *highest attribute* of raw energy, something the ancient sages referred to as awareness, which we now refer to as the spirit.

As mentioned earlier, the mind is primarily designed to function on its own, subconsciously from its memory and intellect from its reckless unconscious thoughts. It gets conditioned with beliefs in identifications and attachments of this and that into its 'me and mine'. Such a prejudiced mind functioning in autopilot takes you on a roller-coaster ride in duality into pairs of opposites to determine and choose for its self-interest, relying basically on beliefs. For this reason, since most opinions differ from one mind to another, conflicts arise, becoming the cause of mess and misery. An ego-self, a thinker emerges in self-consciousness, presuming one's beliefs are superior to others.

In this manner, the human mind on one end represents the psychological self, working from its subconscious section randomly in ego-consciousness. And, on the other, we have the witnessing consciousness (soul) as the saviour, subtly checking upon that ego-self whenever it crosses any limits. The full potentiality of the witnessing self is never realized because the mind is predominantly designed to work from its subconscious section operating under desire and fear, further increasing its recklessness. The primary character of any flow of energy is to expand in randomness unless its flow is checked to evolve into its absoluteness, wholesomeness, or oneness from where it parted to experience something in higher consciousness.

Therefore, despite being that potential divine, the witnessing self remains imprisoned within the mind and is never able to realize its full potentiality of absoluteness in total awareness. There always remains a clash between the desirous ego-consciousness and the witnessing self, and, as evident today, the former seems to be having a decisive edge over the latter. It is only when the presence of any individual awareness—meaning, your true self—is not attached or identified to any thoughts of me and mine, you become free from that dual living in pleasure and pain and celebrate life in its wholesomeness with the body, mind, and spirit. All three flowing as one in harmony. In such moments of now, you are not only aware and conscious but spontaneously proactive to experience and realize without any selfish thoughts.

Since now or the present moment cannot be measured, it has no connection with space or time; the moment of now can have any duration—short or long. In fact, it includes all three—past, present, and future—as one; like in the case of happiness, a dual state of mind. It is during those moments of happiness wherein there is neither desire nor the presence of time. It merely experiences pleasure for that short moment of now, but there is sadness lurking behind like a shadow only to appear later. This is why spiritualism never speaks of happiness, for that is a state of duality and is not for the spirit. The spirit is linked only with the awakening of that true self, and the effortless liberation from desires and attachments to usher in peace instead of happiness for the mind. Only when you witness independently, impartially and impersonally from the body and the cognitive mind, it is during that spontaneous moment of now, the presence of your ego (thinking self) is not attached. You are one with the universe, which, in turn, reveals you are fundamentally none other than the whole of the universe.

Chapter 5

THE THREE LEVELS OF
HUMAN CONSCIOUSNESS

*'You are unconditioned and changeless, formless
and immovable, unfathomable awareness
and unperturbable, so hold to nothing but
consciousness.'*

—John Richards, Ashtavakra Gita (1.17)

THE DECLARATIONS AND DELIBERATIONS MADE BY OUR sages in the subject of spiritualism contain invariably varied personal opinions while translating the quintessence of the Vedantic thoughts from prehistoric Sanskrit, which is different from today. They have been formulated out of our ancient scriptures and have since been sparked by free inquiry open for all speculations. Hence, the subject of Hindu spiritualism has branched out with many representations like in Buddhism, Jainism, Sikhism, etc., each upholding their view, leaving the ground open for any seeker to understand from his or her level of understanding, how, and in what manner one wishes to agree and believe.

Keeping this in mind, I present the decoding of the fundamentals of this subject. The eternal spirit is deliberated as the only supreme primal energy; the highest attribute in the form of total awareness or Paramatma. The soul comes second and is a step lower since it is individualized as Antaratma within the brain of a living creature. It remains separate from the physical body holding the above-mentioned supreme energy to engage in the role of a witnessing self—Sakshi. The third stage is that of *Jivatma*, which identifies with the physical body exerting the body and mind to experience the world of duality in ego-consciousness.

Meaning, from our being-ness arises and matures the form of a transitory being, which further extends into its becoming-ness while we are awake and alive for the eternal energy to expand, experience, and evolve for its evolution. Let me reiterate for the sake of clarity: The spirit is that supreme attribute of energy, which unfolds all that exists in this world. It is that universal force of power, which is infinite and eternal in formless waves of energy, which, in no manner, should be considered as the self. It is that all-important, life-sustaining principle from which everything becomes known. This enlivening and vitalizing force of energy, we refer to as awareness, radiates and shines through its field of consciousness.

Second, the soul or *atman* is that *core energy of an individual self*, which is dependent and supported by supreme energy. Though being impersonal and impartial, it plays the centralized role of making the body and mind aware and, after that, conscious of countering and checking the random flow of unconscious thoughts. It is that link between the personal and the supreme energy (transpersonal). The third is that ego, which is the holding factor of the intellect playing its role of 'mine and yours', experiencing the world in different levels of consciousness for the individual to *become* something in life.

We have three basic levels of consciousness discreetly working in the brain. First is the conscious mind—if and when the mind is alert, it becomes aware and, after that, if attentive, becomes conscious out of all it perceives. It forms our unique individuality depending entirely upon the intensity of its awareness. The mind, in order to become conscious, takes time to focus and concentrate on any object to think, reason, and infer. Subsequently, memory and intellect take over for the mind to go on a roller-coaster ride of its own without being conscious. Like if the mind has learnt something consciously, after that, it goes in an autopilot mode, not requiring the conscious mind to interfere. It relies more on spontaneity (the spirit) because after the mind is aware of the present moment, it intensely penetrates what it perceives, and this is what makes it different from the subconscious state. It is this higher state of consciousness, which can instantaneously capture instinct and intuition and proactively translate that into intelligence for the mind to understand better.

The second level, as mentioned above, is that subconscious section when the mind recalls data from its memory and the intellect, digging out information from its past awareness. At this moment, it functions in an autopilot mode. The subconscious mind is your storehouse, which accumulates, retrieves, and progresses data as and when the brain demands. It works on its own from past knowledge, the memory bank, without any interference from the conscious section. Most decisions are made by the subconscious mind, unconsciously flowing randomly and recklessly, multitasking into this and that in order to facilitate its material mind.

For this reason, in the East, the subconscious mind is said to be asleep, even though awake. Meaning, the mind is not conscious of what is being discharged. The cognitive mind is an operating system of the subconscious stage. Your brain remembers your name, identity, gender, and what it has learnt from its past only because your subconscious says so; you do not require your conscious state for that.

It is the third section, which is responsible for making the mind spiritually aware. It is considered to be that *superconscious* section originating from the unconscious stratum of the brain. It is that layer, which we refer to as the soul, within which the divine spirit of potentially aware energy resides. Its function is merely to *watch, witness, and observe* before any cognitive function—conscious or subconscious.

Many a time, it subtly whispers and warns when the mind is about to cross any limit, making it aware and conscious of its subconscious material wants. The purpose of our spiritual tradition is to *awaken* this spirit lying dormant within to make the mind continuously aware to experience and realize more from its conscious attribute, rather than overly functioning subconsciously in auto mode.

If the mind is not made aware of what it perceives, which is generally the case, the body and the brain exist unconsciously from the subconscious sphere. It is primarily for this reason we come across rampant disorder, despair, and anguish . . . demanding the urgent need for understanding the subject of spiritualism lucidly. Unless there is clarity, knowledge on its own has no meaning, except inflating one's ego.

Therefore, the brain desperately needs to awaken this subtle and astute mechanical system to steer its psychic course of random and reckless chattering in unconscious thoughts, speech, and actions countering that with a conscious approach. Understanding consciousness is the biggest mystery for science to unravel. From the subjective noumenal cosmos, beyond space and time emerges that phenomenal experiential world of space and time, which we refer to as consciousness—the becoming-ness, the consequence of our evolution. The awareness, which activates and enlivens the mind, is ignited by the superconscious section transmitting and receiving from the cosmos in the corresponding frequency that any individual mind vibrates. Please note, human beings are the only known creatures capable of being aware to observe inwardly as well as outwardly upon all that exists in the universe, another reason for being referred to as 'Thou Art That'.

Hence, a human soul, if awakened, possesses limitless potentiality in the becoming of a unique individuality from the infinite awareness, since it is the witnessing self that makes the mind aware and, after that, conscious of what it perceives. The fundamental difference between awareness and consciousness signifies the former to be non-dual and absolute by nature and the latter to be dualistic. It is this infinitude power of awareness in the human mind, which made the ancient sages boldly declare, Aham Brahmasmi—you are the creator and the creation in which the universe resides. It is your limitless power, which can unravel that God and the universe. Hence, the spirit contained in a soul is *identifiable and identical* to the universal spirit of awareness.

Between any stimulus and the mind's response, there is a gap. The brain requires time to respond to any stimulus. Consciousness requires time to imagine, focus, concentrate, and think on what the mind observes. Meaning, when we feel, think and react, self-consciousness comes to the fore. However, when we *pro-act spontaneously* without any feeling, straight from observation into action—meaning, without any thoughts—both the conscious and the subconscious are set aside in a state of choicelessness; the superconscious mind, then, pre-empts with immediate awareness.

In pro-action, there is just the role of observation in primordial awareness initiating immediate activity. In such a state, the mind is still (without any dual thoughts) as well as dynamic in that present moment, choiceless, impersonal, and impartial to any past/future thoughts. Pro-action is for the spiritual-minded—without any analytical thoughts— immediate action without any concern for its results. A reactive mind, on the other hand, is meant for the material— thinking self. It emotionally distinguishes from its desires in duality, with relativity in dichotomies, what it wishes to choose. It is this analysis, which takes time for the material mind, consciously or subconsciously, to choose anything for its self-interest. Mostly, it performs subconsciously from its past cognitive data in selfishness and in separation from its oneness of all that exists.

Pro-action requires no time; there is this presence of immediate aware-conscious energy ready to proceed in any non-dual thought or action. Meaning, if we are mentally free from any emotional or desirous attachments, the presence of awareness immediately determines, *pro-acts*, and experiences from the intensity of its aware energy in the present moment, straight from its superconscious level. Therefore, awareness is that source of immediate intelligence from which we proactively or intuitively determine creative results. Later, if we react, then the mind has time to decide for its material outcome intellectually.

In the other scenario, the moment the primordial awareness continues further into the mind, the thinking self gets activated; fuelled by desires, it takes over and separates the oneness of energy into its duality in relativity to choose, experience, and infer in opposites, say, that of positive or negative. Meaning, in the case of a reaction, the mind identifies and attaches to objects out of desire, clings to them, and becomes emotional about them. Accordingly, our thoughts react to such sensations and the subconscious in an autopilot mode through its intellect and memory decides, discerns, and determines on the direction it wishes to proceed. However, if the mind is focused and attentive on what it perceives, it becomes conscious of its perception and takes time to formulate and experience. We are told by neuroscientists today that the subconscious in an autopilot mode rules the mind by over 95 per cent. The remaining is left for the conscious and the superconscious. The former is subscribed to material living and the latter for the spiritual, giving rise, proportionately, of around 95 per cent growth in materialism and the diminutive for spiritualism.

Now, let us understand the concept of the soul (Atman) and the ego. Both are the same; the former is that of higher consciousness (Antaratma) and the latter is what we refer to as the lower or ego-consciousness (Jivatma). Both comprise forming the individuality of any human being to determine and reflect *what* we are. The spirit entrapped in the soul, on the other hand, constitutes the highest attribute of energy, which we refer to as awareness—that ultimate knowingness, which oversees the mind and body representing itself as the 'I-less' or formless state of being-ness of *who* we are. When the spirit enters a human mind, it embeds in that non-cognitive section, which spiritualists refer to as the superconscious section of the mind.

An *individualized* portion of the universal energy exhibiting its awareness is what we call the soul. The soul is that true self, which radiates within your mind, independently, without having any link to another soul. It is that witness-er, which watches and witnesses via the superconscious section to make the cognitive mind aware and conscious of all that it perceives. In spiritualism, we refer to the soul as Sakshi, the witnessing consciousness. When the witness-er (soul) witnessing (through the mind) conjoins with the witnessed (the object of observation), the mind becomes one with the I-less state of the spirit of *who* we are, fully awakened. In such a state of being-ness, consciousness no longer remains separated; the mind is in total awareness (Chaitanya).

The soul is that link between the personal consciousness and the transpersonal spirit. It is a grade less than the spirit for it is individualized in a human mind. After death, the role of the witnessing soul is over, and it dissipates. The witness (the spirit within) collapses and departs back into its universal abode of nothingness (Shunyata). Please keep in mind, even though the spirit is contained within the soul, it retains its state of absoluteness. It impartially witnesses, via the soul, what the mind does.

Please note, the role of the soul is more of a subject-object relationship between the personal and the universal. It is symbolized with an 'I' to witness its own psychological and physiological self. Meaning, the *soul is not the ultimate; the spirit is*. The spirit is that ultimate subject of '*who we are*' and body, mind, and soul is the object of '*what we are*'—an illusory self, projecting as an individual being to appear and disappear into the nothingness of the universe, where the concept of self simply cannot exist.

On the death of any individual body and mind, the third element—the personal role of the soul—is finally done. Witnessing ends and the subject/object duality in consciousness scatters into the absoluteness of the cosmic energy. What remains at this point is only that awareness or the spirit, which is set free after the death of anybody. Therefore, in the study of self-knowledge, what you need to understand with clarity is that when the self is set free, what remains is that ultimate oneness in absoluteness as no-self; the presence of non-dual absolute energy as the only eternal existence in the universe within which all forms appear and disappear for the duration that they last.

Therefore, you—as the soul in the manner of an independent self with a subject-object relationship—are that witness-er bearing a part of that absolute non-dual cosmic aware energy, which we refer to as the spirit. Meaning, because of holding that supreme energy within the superconscious section, the overall human mind has that potentiality of purity in divinity—referred to as Thou Art That, which always remains enlightened and realized. It is that cognitive mind, the thinking 'I', the material self, functioning separately in duality, which requires transcendence from its lower consciousness in ego to go towards that higher self to evolve and enlighten itself.

What you truly require is to, first, understand and distinguish between the temporary 'I' in physical form (ego-self) and the relationship it carries with the permanent 'I-less' state in formlessness representing as your being-ness. This is made possible by the soul acting between that personal self and the transpersonal spirit. All are real and one in unity and continuity as the substrata of the absolute energy—interpretations and conceptualizations differ because ultimately all that exists can only be one and not two.

Meaning, the unreal cannot exist; they just differ in their interpretations. The impersonal exists as *un-manifested* absolute energy within the soul, and the personal self in the form of *manifested* conscious energy within the cognitive section. Though independent, they are inherent and intrinsic to each other. The subject of spiritualism, for this reason, has been divided into two sections—the higher knowledge (Para Vidya) of the ultimate existence in abstract formlessness, and the lower knowledge (Apara Vidya) into physical forms consisting of all transient existences superimposed on the former.

Therefore, let desires come and go; experience and celebrate, watch and witness, *but do not identify and attach.* Your manifested consciousness will be able to reveal and reflect its true potentiality in totality as it happened in the case of Buddha or Krishna. It will no longer be connected or identified to any duality, whether in materiality or spirituality. Both are conceptual processes of the same mind to engage, evaluate, exercise, experience, and effectuate to evolve in life. Know yourself; you are a part of the presence of that un-manifested spirit of cosmic energy, and your cognition relates only to temporary manifestations of this and that in likes and dislikes. Reactions arise directly out of identifying and attaching to emotional feelings from desires, which, in turn, enhance after receiving further inputs from the intellect and memory to choose in self-interest.

However, if your mind is aware and understands about this space between any two thoughts, you become conscious of what the brain is doing. You are that observation flowing in waves of aware energy, which oversees through an individual soul (observer), merely watching and witnessing with the body and the mind in conformity as one. Therefore, aware consciousness is an application, a movement existing in that space between sensation or impulse and the time taken by the mind to pro-act or react. The same has been further clarified in the subsequent chapters.

Therefore, you are that changeless reality, the presence of observation composed of un-manifested absolute energy, which is free from all bindings. However, when the mind becomes bound to its identity in emotional attachments, reflections of a temporary self in ego-consciousness emerge, which is more from your illusory mind and not the true self. Under the aura of illusions, the material self persists, as explained by Rene Descartes: 'I think, therefore, I am'. However, you are more than that—the subject of observation, observing through the mind on the object being observed. Meaning, 'I am that formless supreme energy, which makes the mind aware and, after that, conscious for the mechanical operation present in the brain to think'.

Spiritual living is to observe clearly. Actual meditation is that effortless movement of observation while observing the inside out. When others provoke, do not react; watch your brain, and you will know precisely what is happening inside your mind. If you respond, you are putting the soul into bondage with that situation. A child is ignorant; the mind observes his or her parents, watching how they react to his or her demands. If they keep succumbing to the child's whims and fancies, consciousness develops in a crooked manner. He or she, as the soul/observer, gets imprisoned as a victim in a vicious cycle of pleasure and pain condemning and demanding from his or her life, this or that. The ego emerges, the thinker enlarges, and the individual mind unconsciously flows subconsciously, always wanting but never fulfilled.

Therefore, please remember, a human being—irrespective of representing itself as a god, guru, or disciple—so long as one is composed within an independent body, mind, and soul, will remain separated in dual living, hence, incomplete. One may attain higher consciousness, but the absoluteness in oneness can only be realized when all three—body, mind, and soul—dematerialize, dissolving as one.

Desire is that fuel of the mind, which is designed to move only in duality to choose what it wants in relativity through opposites for its illusory self. Anything that materializes within a limited space and time, like consciousness, remains partial and unfinished due to its separation in duality. However, the *absolute* awareness of the spirit, which endures and persists untouched by any such desires—unrelated to space or time—is that ultimate, one and only god responsible to make the mind aware and conscious. It remains birthless and deathless and is that whole and immortal. It is that potential untainted energy settled in the superconscious section of the human brain entrapped in a soul, which we refer to as the witnessing self or consciousness.

I repeat, aware energy (spirit) within the soul is total and complete. It is that primordial awareness, which provides bursts of fresh energy responsible for delivering unique intelligence and individual creativity to the intellect. The moment thoughts arise, it extends and separates; the mind becomes aware and conscious to analyze, experience, choose, and infer. Meaning, awareness later expands into thoughts of duality, which separates the non-dual energy into opposites, and the same aware structure now from its conscious or subconscious field of energy, ready to experience the dualities of life. Primordial or spontaneous awareness is that manifestation of absolute energy restricted to what we refer to as instinct, intuition, or natural intelligence. It is that basic understanding of *common sense* of every individual, which you should respect. Do not challenge this divine intelligence as it is far superior to your imaginative intellect consisting of past and borrowed knowledge from here and there.

Watch and witness your dual operating mind. It will continue to chatter in random thoughts, multitasking in greed, separating the absolute energy through its intellect into its opposites of good and bad, positive and negative, and so on. The benefit of witnessing arises subtly and effortlessly while you watch and witness; the mind becomes shy and conscious and starts to correct itself. If you wish for fulfilment in life, make all the amends to bring these separated forms of energies of materiality and spirituality closer towards their oneness because, without one, the other cannot exist. Like without the devil, God cannot exist. Both belong to unitary absolute energy, separated into two, by the mind.

If your mind is aware only of the outside, the inner self remains confined. It is total only if and when you are alert to watch and witness making your mind aware of its past awareness . . . inside as well as outside. When you react, your mind remains unconscious, directed more towards material attachments bound to the outside. However, when it is alert and aware, in and out, you spontaneously pro-act from within to tackle any situation. The mind is split between the inner and the outer—the inner radiates in oneness towards higher consciousness. The outer, affected by the environment, drags the mind towards the lower material consciousness in emotional desires and attachments. How you interact and balance these two is the art of living.

Please remember, when you look at the mirror, you see the reverse image. Similarly, the world we perceive is an inversion of the actual. However, when you observe inwards, the intensity of your awareness awakens, radiating your true self through its consciousness—indicating the reflection that you see in the mirror is that illusory self, which is more of an optical illusion.

Allow me to explain this again: The image that you see in the mirror does not exist. It is merely a temporary component of multiple forms of condensed energy vibrating in different frequencies, like many other objects that you see and feel. According to quantum science, many believe there is no such thing as matter. Both matter and energy can be converted into each other. Energy, when dormant like in the case of dark energy, is only a wave. However, when light energy moves, vibrates, and reverberates in myriad frequencies, it can behave both as a wave and a particle, depending upon how they are observed. The reason, it has now become *aware*. All those are probability waves, which merely appear as solid to any brain, which is not able to perceive a wave as a wave. Meaning, there has to be another subtler wave before the probability wave, which oversees both a wave and a particle. The ancient sages referred to this subtle mystical principle as the highest attribute of energy that we today refer to as the spirit.

Therefore, just the noumenal state of being-ness (awareness) exists, for, in actuality, there is no physical being but only potential waves of energy, which can reflect as a particle as and when it wishes. The phenomenal body and mind do not have any permanent existence, something that is prone to constant changes from one shape to another like you see in the mirror. These are just superimposed on the true nature of your reality that temporarily appears to exist. As you know, reflections do not affect the mirror in any manner. Correspondingly, body, mind, and emotions—whatever they reflect for a short while—cannot affect the true nature of reality. Thus, we have two separate realities—absolute (ultimate) and relative (dual); the former is real and the latter merely a reflection of the real.

The mind, unconsciously through blind beliefs, conceptualizes images of personal gods, heaven and hell, and all sorts of dual characteristics; attaching itself to property, name, gender, nationality, etc., depending on its degree of beliefs. It visualizes and imagines around those beliefs, making them rigid and extreme. These preconceived ideas later become conditioned and prejudiced, maturing into faith, which the mind takes them to be real. Therefore, life revolves around such rigid illusions, without the mind knowing how to ascertain and establish its actual nature of the self. Beliefs, which are generally not verifiable, become your reality, which is not true.

You are the presence of that pure, aware energy in its being-ness, just watching, through mind, the temporary forms of interchangeable sub-energies representing their attributes. What you witness may go against your mind's prejudiced ideology and the images of the world that it carries. Eventually, it is your spiritual intelligence that determines the inner truth. Furthermore, conflicts arise when your beliefs differ from one to another—you argue to prove you are right and the other wrong, and as a result, ego emerges. We have no other recourse but to awaken that inner spirit and be free from such distortions in illusory beliefs and bindings. Otherwise, the mind continues to spin around a roller-coaster ride of happiness and sadness, not knowing how to get out of such a rigmarole.

Physicists keep looking and observing, presuming physical objects to be real. Spiritually, we need to understand with clarity what the true nature of reality is and not what you see objectively and measure. The nature of absolute energy is that unchanging, eternal source or the subject of everything that exists, constant and indivisible, which can neither be created nor destroyed, being complete in all respects as the whole. Shanti Mantra has well projected the said principle on the nature of the ultimate reality from prehistoric times, which has now been confirmed by the law of conservation of energy. Absolute energy is the substratum of all matter and consciousness. On its own, it remains constant; however, within it expresses and exhibits various forms of subset and interchangeable energies that superimpose on the real while they appear and disappear. It is that universal unity in continuity, if seen by the senses, it seems finite; it is in sheer awareness that comprehends the same in its infinite grandiose.

The reality, of course, is one without a second, unchanging and eternal with zero constraints of space and time, but the mind needs to be aware and, after that, become conscious of apprehending this nature with clarity and authenticity. Relative reality may change from one to another depending upon space, time, and causation, but their intrinsic absolute state will always reveal as one and unchanging. The nature of absolute reality has its subjective dimension in the eternal form of awareness. The objective measurements in temporary forms of matter and consciousness merely confirm as many behind the one ultimate reality.

Therefore, *being of any finite object* is nothing but a superimposition on the infinite being-ness of the absolute energy as the only existence, as it is, the way it is, unchanging and real. However, energy also has this tendency to expand, evolve, and effectuate, which the ancient sages referred to as Brahman (to grow). It grows circularly to *become* something undergoing constant evolution . . . where the death of anything is only the beginning of new birth. In this evolutionary process, *becoming conscious of the self* becomes more relevant than its force of aware being. So, hold on to your consciousness, become something out of your uniqueness, so that you may leave something behind as a legacy for all to remember when your body and mind are no longer there. *Becoming* is that meaning and purpose of life, while your profound mind is active and alive.

Chapter 6

THE NATURE OF BEING
AND BECOMING

'You are not earth, water, fire or air. Nor are you
empty space.
Liberation is to know yourself as Awareness
alone—the Witness of these.'
—Bart Marshall, Ashtavakra Gita (1.3)

To BE IS TO EXIST, *BEING* IS THE ESSENTIAL NATURE, and *becoming* is that process to develop into something. Becoming initiates a change in what exists, say, from a state of formlessness to a state of temporary self of living in body and mind. This chapter speculates how we misrepresent our 'I', the self that we consider to be the 'me and mine'. In the subject of spiritualism, the essential nature of what we believe as our being is an illusion. Body and mind are more about becoming something temporarily and are not our actual reality. We exist more in the presence of a state of being-ness, where there is no 'I', self, or anything physical, personal, or material. Being reflects a certain *quantity* in body and brain, whereas being-ness radiates the presence and the intensity of our *quality*.

Our actual reality is a state of that non-dual wave of energy, which is always present in the eternal now that reflects a *qualification* of being aware. Whatever exists in the universe, from stars to subatomic particles, become our observable reality only after we are aware. The presence of this awareness is our being-ness, which unfolds and unravels all that we see or hear from our sensory organs. Meaning, what we see is seen only after we become aware of the same. Meaning, nothing can exist unless we are aware of it—exemplifying our being-ness in the form of awareness, the quality of *who we are*, which, of course, is far more critical than the quantity of *what we are*.

Why does a human mind, despite being so phenomenal, run amuck in randomness, edgy and anxious in a state of chaos, repeatedly victimized under the mercy of materiality? All because of one simple reason, the brain is ignorant about its true self (quality); it presumes that quantum of accumulated thoughts to be its 'I am—this and that'. Furthermore, science, too, is ignorant about the same. The mind, in order to know its actual master, has no other option but surrender to the paranormal powers of the noumenal spirit. Thus, the human mind is simply not aware, neither of its actual reality nor of what the true nature of existence is all about.

The nature of subjective reality supersedes that of the factual, observable, comprehensible, empirical, or measurable ever-changing objective reality. Reality encompasses far more than what we perceive; it is absolute and unchanging, one without a second. It is subjective and not objective, eternal, or infinite in its true essence, like the sky we perceive. The reason, anything that keeps changing in space and time or with cause and effect cannot be considered as permanent reality; it is relative, short-lived, and dependent. Mind, on the other hand, is dualistic by nature and perceives what it *believes* to be real and that, too, limited to space and time. Therefore, please remember the 'I Am' existing in body and mind is only a transient objective reality effectuated by the emergence of a conscious principle in the precincts of the phenomenal mind, superimposed on the absolute subjective reality—the substratum of all that exists . . . the noumenal in total awareness.

A spiritual seeker, seeking the sought is, in fact, going on a pathless path because he himself *is* what he seeks—total awareness. In the search for truth, there is no path for us to apply nor any efforts, methods, or techniques to experience and realize. Awareness is both the cause and effect of everything. Life is merely a play for that subjective awareness to *observe, watch, and witness* how your body and mind in duality is experiencing and realizing the objective (mid-reality) in this and that from the perception of its senses to become something from its being-ness while it is active and alive.

For that matter, enlightenment also is simply an experiential process of the mind that will eventually mature and realize. When all knowledge comes to an end, what remains is only the truth in the eternal now expressing its nothingness in Shunyata. Hence, becoming of any existence is more philosophical where the individual being-ness (uniqueness) brings about the possibility of a change in a thing (body and mind) that has a temporary life (vibrations of energy) in it, something that is regarded more as an illusion and not reality. Science, too—relying upon ancient philosophies—hides behind consciousness to provide us with tools to enhance or refine age-old doctrines, giving rise to further speculations and arguments.

So, for the human mind to be awake and alive, authentic spiritualists emphasize more upon the metaphysical spirit of *awareness* rather than those subconscious thoughts, which create havoc in your mind. And, for that metaphysical becoming, consciousness has been endorsed and empowered to sum up your individuality of *what you are* at any given space and time. Of course, over and above that false persona, your external personality portrays. Consciousness in its simple decoding refers to *responsive awareness*, inner and outer, when the mind responds to what it is aware.

Consciousness is that wakefulness, which forms your individuality, disposing of your nature as the ego-self as well as the subtle witnessing one. It is the screen of that inner theatre, which reveals your outer personality and, at the same time, reflects your inner individuality. Consciousness sums up your inherent characteristics from its conscious, subconscious, and superconscious subsections. It is that inner construct of the mind and not supernatural in any manner, as presumed by many. It is the total of the subconscious (unconscious thoughts), conscious (attentive thoughts), and superconscious (thoughtless observation) connected to the mind's functioning in duality to discern, differentiate, and decipher one out of the two in relativity with opposites—say, between God and the devil.

The subject of spirituality relates basically to the processes of the senses—how to discipline the thinking mind? It provides reformative methods and techniques to quiet the mind from its constant chatter. However, these motivational efforts are not fruitful in their totality because they are temporary. The mind bounces back to its material essence with extra vigour from its ego-self. It is the subject of spiritualism (the higher knowledge), which goes beyond the mind, into the core—the spirit—to elucidate the true nature of reality as one without a second, which subsumes all that temporarily exists, superimposed on its ultimate reality.

The subject of spiritualism takes up the nature of reality metaphysically—material and immaterial—in the forms of matter and consciousness. The subject subtly conveys that thoughts will always reign supreme in mind; they cannot be directly quieted or suppressed. In the becoming of our material world, our being-ness is influenced by feelings, thoughts, intention, attitude and faith all because of desires of what you see, perceive, and believe. However, with respect to the nature of your true being-ness, you are that abstract, formless wave of spiritual energy going through human experiences. In such a scenario, even human gods become questionable in their absolute reality. Meaning, the reality is illusory when you mentally perceive through your senses and is accurate when you go beyond the mind.

Since all that exists is only energy, the force of energy in our case remains dormant in its state of absoluteness, without being aware of itself. However, when this *force* settles in the human brain, it enables the individual mind to become aware and, after that, conscious in order to radiate its field of power in the form of consciousness. As mentioned earlier, in the spiritual context, this individualized potential force of absolute energy, which we refer to as the soul, is considered to be a notch less than the universal spirit of total awareness. It radiates in separation from its universality and has been designated as the 'witnessing self or consciousness'. It is that absolute state of superconsciousness within any individual mind, which occurs in silence with choiceless and thoughtless thoughts, enabling the mind to become spontaneously aware.

In short, when un-manifested, absolute cosmic energy manifests in mind, it makes the mind aware and conscious with the result activating it to operate through neural pathways via thoughts, memory, and intellect. Going beyond the mind into the spiritual realm relates to those moments when it merely observes what Jiddu Krishnamurti suggested in choiceless awareness. During this moment the mind is not connected to any specific space, time, or any analytical thoughts but pure observation.

In these moments, the brain plays no role while processing this neural impulse, which, after extending, makes the mind aware and conscious to think and experience. Such moments are spontaneous, creative, instinctive, intuitive, and immediate. Intense observation demands from the cosmic energy to enlighten the mind. And those who agree with this phenomenon, exclaim: 'Bingo! I've got it!', which we refer to as eureka.

Consciousness is considered to be paramount by many scientists as well as spiritualists because all revelations on the nature of its observable reality mature and reflect through its field of becoming-ness in body and mind. It plays multiple roles in the forms of super-subconscious and conscious states, which have been extensively elaborated in this book. However, the spirit of total awareness, that absolute non-dual energy embedded in the superconscious section, is that force behind consciousness, which is responsible for making the mind, first, aware and, then, conscious of perceiving what it captures, extending into thoughts of duality in its conscious and subconscious states.

Like the sun, the spirit also is not aware of its potential force of energy. But when the sun radiates its field of light energy, it *becomes* that fundamental source of life on whatever surface it illuminates. Similarly, if the field of consciousness did not exist, nature and objective existence of the universe could not bring about that evolution in any becoming-ness for the energy to expand and evolve—the gradual progression that we see over a long period from genus *Homo* emerging into the modern *Homo sapiens*.

Therefore, the nature of your physical existence is revealed through your personality, the essence of your mental self is reflected through that individuality of your consciousness, and the spiritual core from that awakening of your being-ness in awareness. As mentioned earlier, awareness on its own is not aware of itself. Still, consciousness is aware of its past awareness and is capable of becoming aware and, in turn, conscious of all that exists in this universe. It remains submerged in the objective self, possessing that potentiality to unravel the universe.

The human mind is the most profound and miraculous software one can ever perceive or conceive. However, besides the conscious principle to activate its physical senses, it also requires a master; otherwise, it subconsciously functions in autopilot. To tame the mind, what you need is to make the mind conscious of its acts, and for that, you do not require the memory or the intellect. What you require is that absolute spirit of aware energy—the potential divine seated within the soul, which is the source and the force with the power to make the mind *awake, aware, and conscious* of what it is about to perceive.

Thus, awareness is that force, which radiates a field of consciousness. The highest attribute of the universal energy is awareness, and the ultimate substrate of this energy within the human mind is determined from the soul as the absolute witnessing consciousness. The inherent features of consciousness symbolize a field of metaphysical activity, which science is yet to understand fully. It flows through neural pathways of the brain, simultaneously coexisting as the witnessing self on one end and as that ego-self on the other.

In the former self, this individual flow of energy is not identified or attached to anything impartially witnessing as that true impersonal self, which we refer to as the soul. In the latter or the ego-self, the same field of energy disperses and dissipates amid a persona immersed in a field of an illusory thinking self with a distinct identity, materially attached to this or that with its likes and dislikes to form its false personality.

All physical activities of the body and mind require the fuel of desire and the memory to make it move. For material life, you first need to evaluate and then choose from its dual aspect to fulfil what consciousness desires. However, for the spiritual or that impersonal presence, you merely need to *watch and witness* the inside, meaning, your mind to awaken the presence of that individual sleeping spirit (total awareness) in order to make the mind aware and conscious. So long the mind is subconsciously immersed in identifications and attachments to external feelings in desires, the soul remains weak and inactive. In such situations, which is usually the case, the thinking or that ego-self becomes active and consequently gets excessively bound to materiality. In this state of mind, consciousness is never at ease and remains imbalanced.

Therefore, one may have all the wealth, knowledge, family, and comfort, yet there will remain something amiss, unless the dormant spirit awakens to administer a balanced approach between the spiritual and the material. Please keep in mind, motivations navigate desire, and on the other end, it is *contentment*, which initiates solitude, silence, and stability, gradually transcending the mind towards the spirit on a higher citadel of being aware and conscious.

When energy vibrates, it moves randomly, so is the case within the mind. First are those sensations or feelings leading to thoughts, after that, desires mature. The intention of the cognitive mind is always connected to want. The soul, however, is fully coupled to awareness as one in non-duality. Both continue to develop your self-consciousness, where your personal life revolves around who takes the lead—desire or self-awakening. Meaning, the moment any thought configures a sensation, hope or desire predominates. Mostly, desire takes over subconsciously, taking you on a roller-coaster ride of pleasure and pain.

However, between desire and action, there is a space for that observatory self. Always be alert to observe your desires before initiating any action. Desire on its own is not damaging; it is that attachment towards those desires which is. The moment mind is aware of what it desires, it becomes conscious to think and evaluate, either to succumb or to restraint. *The art of life is to continuously witness your inner mind from the middle of your thoughts interposed between self-awareness and desires.*

In the course of an awakening of the soul, there is no distinction between the observer (subject), observing (mind) on the observed (object of sensation). Inside out, they are one (non-dual while witnessing)—the actual self/spirit awakens only during this movement of observation. The potentiality of witnessing is that ability to see things as they are, without any demand, reason, or prejudice. . . in total freedom with purity, without analytical thoughts. Meaning, whether you are seeing or listening, you, as the observer, are uninvolved and unaffected—absorbed as one with the observed.

Thus, the observer is in total accord with the observed during the process of observing from the mind, and this is made possible only during the *present* moment in its primordial awareness. For, say, if the observer is watching in a discriminatory manner from his or her past knowledge, seeking a conclusion or its outcome in the future, that would be more of *analytical thinking* rather than observing freedom.

Everything that manifests in our world is a movement of energy in the present; the future is a continuation of the past, controlled and reconstructed by the present through observation, which has been well elaborated by science—the observer effect where mere observation of a phenomenon inevitably changes that phenomenon. This happens when the observation is taking place without any supposition, assumption, reasoning, or judgement, and there is totality; no fragmentation into this or that, the past is trying to learn something anew for its future in the *present*.

The mind requires the memory and intellect to recollect the past, move further, and grow to evolve for its future. The only difference here is that during primordial observation, the movement is non-dual, always in the present in its absoluteness, without any thinking. It results in making the mind aware and, after that, conscious of its observation. When this movement extends into the psychological mind, analytical thoughts emerge to separate the absoluteness into its duality in order to analyze, choose, experience, and infer out of its biased beliefs.

Thoughts are always of the past, arising from memory, and after that reasoned from the intellect. The mind now subconsciously goes into action in an autopilot mode after obtaining its required data from its past awareness. Say, if a question is asked, the mind recollects from its memory, reasons from its intellect, and answers. Thus, in that space between a thinker and the thought, there is a presence of a conditioned mind based on past beliefs, which leads to conflict and misery because every mind is conditioned differently according to their personal taste, opinions, and experiences.

Meaning, once the mind has observed and learnt after a particular experience, it feels it is confident in performing independently, without being conscious of how and what it performs. Based on past beliefs, mind imitates, borrows, and reacts from its prejudiced conditioned mind, not requiring the conscious section. It is for this reason that the human mind overly performs from its subconscious section—the reason for seeing imbalances all around. Therefore, the solution lies not only from what you observe but also understanding with clarity: 'I am that Awareness', which provides all the answers to make the mind aware, conscious, and stable from its random and reckless subconscious movements.

When you practise meditation, there is a specific motivation, desire, or intention coming from that thinking mind, which nullifies the whole practice, binding your mind to what it desires. Meditate as often as you can, every moment; but do it with sheer observation, not as a doer, motivated through the mind, but in silent watchfulness. Because in actual meditation, there should be no presence of any doer or meditator. Both meditation and samadhi are states of a 'non-thinking mind'. If you practise varying thoughts or through breathing exercises, you defeat the purpose of being present with your spiritual self. You do not need to *practise* meditation or samadhi to realize your true spiritual self; you are already that. All you require is to be alert, continuously observe, and witness the mind to remind you of what you already are. True samadhi is when you do not feel anything, and you do not experience anything being in that state of thoughtlessness without any identifications or attachments.

The body and mind are those probable quantum wave fields of energy potentially manifesting or condensing into gross energy as matter and subtle in consciousness, materializing in space and time to vanish gradually after that. Any wave of energy without the force-field attribute is sheer nothing; awareness is that centrifugal force from which its field of consciousness emerges. It is that mysterious subject, prior and above the raw energy, causeless from space and time, and the one and only reality we refer to as the spirit. After that, ego-consciousness takes over to satiate its desires, overly experiencing material life. On the other end, to counter this excessive behaviour, what you have is that witnessing consciousness in total awareness, the core, which represents your soul. Keep watching and witnessing your mind; it shall come closer and closer towards that centre, which will neutralize that excessive materiality with *spiritual-ness*.

All psychic efforts in subconscious beliefs will only lead towards conflicts; especially when that illusory thinking mind exercises them. The spirit neither evaluates, condemns nor judges; it merely watches and witnesses. The moment you are out of such a spiritual state, you get bound and persist in illusions with beliefs and faith of the past. There is nothing unusual in that becoming because that is more for the material life wanting to accumulate all that it can. Passively, without any efforts, discover who is inside. That true self, hidden within your mind, is what guides you towards that wholesome *becoming*, enabling you to balance between the spiritual and the material with clarity, consistency, and contentment in humility.

Therefore, if you think you are the mind, you will remain a slave of your beliefs. However, if you know, you are not the mind but more than the mind, you become a master of that mind. Belief is frivolous, continually changing with time and space. It is an idea, which you try to share, force, and convince others of what you know. Likewise, faith is rigid in deep belief, tough to change even if evidence emerges, creating doubt on its authenticity. When you have a belief or opinion, it provides no factuality. But when you have faith, you become determined to follow what you believe, whether it is correct or not. So, be very careful, observe and witness both your mind and what it believes or has faith in, candidly and freely as both strongly interplay with each other in life. Do not believe in what I write, use your own intelligence; your mind should always remain open and free to what it understands with clarity.

I repeat, when your mind is merely observing, you are in a state of thoughtlessness; there is no thinking, no choice, and no analysis, just simple observation. It is focused in the now;

the duration is timeless. In those present moments, there is no resistance whatsoever. From one moment to the next, the brain is in an active state of proactivity, where thoughts are still and dynamic at the same time. It is neither chattering recklessly nor multitasking.

Activity in the present moment is essential for any spiritual seeker because, at that moment, the mind is creative and free. There is an absence of any manipulative or reactive thoughts to disturb the present moment. With the result, you have no impulses of attachment to desire, and the cognitive mind becomes passive and still. Otherwise, calculative thoughts go into action, producing emotions of likes and dislikes. The material mind swings from the past into the future, ignoring the present. Like a pendulum, it depends from one end to another, not bothering to pause or stop at the centre, which is the present.

A proactive mind is free and flows with the least resistance. It operates for the material as well as the spiritual. In a reactive state, emotions get involved and in self-interest tilt more towards the outside, a world in which one materially lives, sustains, and survives for the sake of the body with an analytical mind deviously playing for its selfishness.

However, within this temporary thinking self, there also exists a microcosm of the universe, eternal and infinite, which, in our case, we refer to that as the spirit (total awareness). Most of us know a lot about the material self because it provides immediate results for the betterment of our mind and body in terms of wealth and comfort. However, if we do not make enough effort to know and understand the spiritual self, life remains incomplete and unfulfilled. The result is evident from the despair, hopelessness, and depression we see around.

The material provides the mind with fulfilment for attaining this and that, whereas in spiritual pursuit, mind neither accomplishes nor accumulates anything. The mind simply recognizes its true self; it acknowledges and becomes alert on the qualitative aspect of its true presence. In turn, it makes your mind aware and conscious of how it can keep its material rhapsody in check. The mind should always be centred between the material and the spiritual. Both are essential to experience life. Despite being opposites, both interact with each other, the formless and the form as one and not two. The mind requires aware spiritual energy to perceive and conceive all that it can to observe rationally, know, understand, experience, and realize what dualities of life is all about in its totality and not in fragments.

It is that absolute spiritual aware energy going through the relative material experience. In ignorance, the mind becomes more involved comparing itself with others rather than evolving from its attachments. The moment the mind desires, it emotionally clings and attaches, identifying with the body and mind. As mentioned earlier, there is nothing to accomplish from this emptiness of nothing since the physical is temporary and passes from one form of energy to another. The mind, on the other hand, needs to become aware of this innate spiritual energy . . . of how unconsciously it takes you on a roller-coaster ride with unpredictable changes revolving around lust and greed. All these factors instil doubt, fear, and insecurity. Subconsciously, you run helter-skelter, blindly following what others tell you to follow, losing your intelligence, and merely imitating what and whom your mind believes.

Fundamentally, there are two types of emotions—fear and love. Around 80 per cent of our thoughts are from fear and the balance from love. If there were no fear, our thoughts would not need to go into the past. The past reminds us of what can happen tomorrow. Moreover, the moment I think from my mind, fear subtly enters, and I wonder how I can protect and preserve all that the mind feels it can possess forever. Incessant desires emerge to fulfil emotional insecurity. However, in actuality, what is truly required is, 'I am neither this body nor the mind. I am that qualified presence of awareness, which is passive and asleep and knows no fear. It comprises boundless love; all that it demands is for the mind to awaken this sleeping tiger to flow freely without any hesitations of "me and mine".

Since the heart is directly connected to a relationship with cause and effect; what you feel and experience in mind immediately has its impact on the heart. The element of emotions differs in every sensation according to that situation. The rate of one's heartbeat further determines the tolerance level in each individual. Like in any similar situation, two different people will reveal different states of behaviour.

Therefore, it is how one reacts to any feeling that determines its intensity of fear; two separate persons in the same situation will reveal different intensities of anxiety in some way or another, connected to future thoughts, wanting either this or that. Sorrows emanate from attachments and fear arises from attachments as well. If the attachment is absent, both disappear. Hence, fear arises from thoughts, which cling to you hoping or wanting something in the future. If wants are reduced, fear reduces as well.

The mind always wishes to attach to more wants, more knowledge, more of everything. The more you read, the more knowledge you get. However, say, in a class or a group study, all students are given the same knowledge, but the degree of understanding differs from one to another; some understand more, while others know less of the same subject. In spiritualism, understanding with clarity is of the essence; it requires more intelligence rather than the intellect to comprehend the *abstract* nature of the spirit. Knowledge increases the intellect; understanding intensifies that intelligence.

Therefore, every knowledge is first required to be understood clearly before you apply experience to it . . . realize and gain wisdom from it. Intellect is past knowledge of what you have gathered or experienced from here and there. It is only after understanding that you become existentially aware and conscious of what you know. Knowledge will make you a believer, master, artiste, or a scholar—all required for the material mind. However, spontaneous intelligence through sheer observation and understanding will make you a discoverer or a creator. You need experiential knowledge for the material self and existential intelligence for that spiritual being-ness. Otherwise, you merely remain an ignorant part of any group, following and imitating some guru or another, repeating Sanskrit jargon to impress others on your borrowed knowledge.

I repeat, knowledge is of no use if it is not correctly understood, experienced, and realized. Both the spirit (intelligence) and the mind (intellect) coincide; they combine to provide that completeness you require for the proper understanding of any subject. Intellect on its own through knowledge provides fodder to the ego. It will only propel you further into darkness. More the knowledge, higher is that ignorance of what you are not. The thinking mind enters into an illusion and imposes on itself the impression 'I know more than you do', when in reality, it does not. The mind at this moment is in a worse situation; it exists in an illusory state of imitating other's knowledge and experiences, projecting what it superficially knows to satiate its ego.

To be spiritual, you are constantly required to watch this material mind, which thrives in duality for its self-interest. Awareness consumes both, the inner as well as outer, with care and love for all as one—a balance that you have become spiritual. After reading a few spiritual books or listening to a few spiritual discourses, one feels that he or she has become spiritual. Spiritualism is a highly complex subject, which requires dedication without any personal reasoning. You need to study this as an independent subject like you would for any other topic.

Very often, only your thoughts lead your mind towards the feeling that you have become spiritual. Spiritual-ness has to reflect without your knowing or boasting about it. Meaning, you as that true self need not become aware of being aware. You *are* that awareness; only your mind needs to become aware and conscious. Your awareness has to be effortless for others to observe. You should always keep in mind that you are a spiritual being going through the human experience of separation in duality.

In religion or transcendental meditation, there is always discipline. The mind is that disciple, which focuses and makes efforts to practise and experience. A desire emerges, and you have an idea what the outcome is going to be, that is, if you practise hard. It is more of a success story and cannot be called transformation. To be spiritual, be qualified in the presence of your awareness in the now; do not attempt to do anything. Your constant observation will prevent your mind from that subconscious desiring in an unconscious manner. Do not cheat that divine residing within. It will subtly warn you of any wrongful, obsessive, or excessive act. After that, it is left to your thinking self whether it wishes to listen to the spirit or towards that desire lurking beneath.

If you wish to know yourself, be yourself; no discipline, practice, or motivation is required because they are more for disciplining the mind rather than awakening that spirit. After going through all those practices, the mind invariably bounces back into the same egoistic world of material and emotional thoughts. Just be yourself; simply be alert. Watch and witness your body and mind constantly, ignoring what you know and desire. Be who you are . . . nothing but the presence of total awareness. Accept with grace your shadow— the alter ego—meaning, the illusory self, whether it is good or bad; just become aware of the same.

Do not *detach* from any of your good or bad habits, for that would be tinkering with the mind. Learn the art of *non-attachment* through observation turning into awareness; watch and witness the mind, and on its own, mind becomes conscious, effortlessly shirking off those habits that are not favourable to your spiritual insight. To further this process, be *content* and that, in return, shall reduce desires on their own and attachments, as a result, will decrease. All attachments arise out of that intensity of desire.

Desire is bound to exist since it is the fuel for the mind—keep watching, leave desire alone, and allow the mind to act on it freely. Either the mind will initiate action on that desire or, without any effort, reject it. The moment you feel and become emotional (thoughts in motion) about that desire, attachment arises. Be neutral. Neither for this nor for that, not even for any desire; just watch and witness, and see how your mind becomes aware to effortlessly decide whether that desire is meant to be fulfilled. The above phenomenon is loosely spoken by many when they say 'go *inwards*' without knowing how to do so.

The moment you feel for any desire, the thinking mind enters. So, do not feel, do not think, just watch and observe. In this manner, you enter into that stillness, which you notice deep below in the ocean, far below the waves where the water is calm and still. It is this particular state of mind, which you require. All anxieties, attachments, and sufferings are those turbulent waves hitting those boulders because of your feelings, thinking, and attaching to satiate desires, creating bondage and fear. Become free from all this, and you will effortlessly go towards enlightenment. Just watch your mind doing all that it does without your involvement, meaning, become impersonal and impartial.

You become free. Everything is happening on its own, like ripples of waves colliding against each other on the surface. Deep down in that ocean (super-consciousness) is where you are; discover that 'you' and your mind shall have peace and tranquillity from that forever wanting material self.

Chapter 7

WHAT DOES IT MEAN TO BE SPIRITUAL?

'Child, you are pure awareness, nothing less.
You and the world are one. So, who are you to
think?
You can hold on to it, or let it go?
How could you!'

—Paramahansa Yogananda, Ashtavakra Gita
(15.12)

IT IS COMMONLY SAID, IN ORDER TO BE SPIRITUAL, YOU need to go inside. But how does one *'go inside'* when one's mind is not adequately answered? Let us first start with what does 'being spiritual' mean? It is that insight, which you alone need to discover from that inner silence that takes you beyond thoughts. It is that ability to live fully, without any distinction between material and spiritual. It is to explore that god within your body and mind, and not outside. It is to recognise that you are a spiritual being going through a human experience. It is to go beyond your thinking being into that spiritual being-ness where you question less and observe more. It is not to *know* but to *understand* that truth: You are much more than body and mind . . . you are the universe.

To be spiritual is to be in a state of *selfless* self, beyond the constraints of that selfish form. In simple terms, when your mind is sensitive towards all as one, you are your true self. Thus, if you wish to experience life without fear, being spiritual is the answer.

Being spiritual is to be free from your cognitive mind, where you are neither attached nor identified to your body or mind. You remain calm and still *continuously watching and witnessing the brain in all its doings*; not attached to anything. When there is no feeling, thought, discipline, practice, or effort for the sake of 'me and mine', the mind dissolves and the spirit awakens. The soul, in turn, observes your mind and body doing everything in self-consciousness. In spirituality, your mind is required to be alert, attentive, self-aware, and conscious to be free from all distortions and prejudices.

So, how does one become spiritual?

First, we need to clearly understand and distinctively accept all three aspects of our composition—body, mind, and soul. The understanding of this triad is imperative, but unfortunately, the third crucial factor is generally ignored by most. No one seems to know what is the soul/spirit or being spiritual is all about? The spirit is *who* we are, consciousness reflects *what* we are, and the body and mind reveal *how* we are. Spirit is that absolute awareness contained in a soul. It is that formless and impersonal being-ness from which your mind becomes impartially aware. It happens to know whatever it knows about the universe and all that exists in its infinitude. Hence, the soul is that observer, which merely watches and witnesses through the spirit on the other two aspects—body and mind.

The mind experiences all pleasure and pain due to that feeling of being a *doer*. It is this doership, which binds the consciousness to the mind's identity and emotional attachments, going through all sorts of pain and suffering. Witnessing is to be a sheer *onlooker* of every sensation to situations, unaffected and uninvolved. We have to be centred in the spirit and identify with the soul, instead of the body-mind nexus. If your mind gets affected and gets involved in any sensation, say, from hunger emerging from the body, it means you are attached to that sensation.

If you remain unaffected and uninvolved, the soul is free, remaining virtuous in choiceless witnessing. There is neither attraction nor repulsion. You become free from past karmas and destiny, duality as well as causation without any likes and dislikes, not clinging to anything to which the mind binds itself. Like in business, if you are not anxious, agitated, or excited from profits or losses, consciousness becomes free from those karmas of the mind. Otherwise, in every sense, you are destined from past actions; but being a witness, you break that link and are free. You befit your true self—spiritual.

Therefore, when you are not bound to any identification or attachments—remaining merely as a witness—you are spiritual, otherwise you are not. Please remember the spirit is forever free and not limited to any space, time, or causation. After entering the mind, it remains dormant unless awakened, and this happens only if the mind is alert and attentive. It is that insight, which is not dependent on any knowledge, methods, exercise, nor on experience, memory, or intellect. Consequently, your individual soul awakens and the mind gets activated spontaneously by sheer observation or witnessing. To be spiritual is to allow the soul to be independent of your mind residing within. In simple terms, though difficult to comprehend, being spiritual involves a) self-knowledge b) self-observation and c) self-awakening where spirit is universal and the soul is that individual observing self. This book centres on that. Here are the three stages of self-observation:

- **First Stage:** Be aware of the *inner* and the *outer* in silence. Endeavour to understand this complex statement—*the presence of awareness is the awareness of that presence.* The mind is required to become aware; you as that observer/soul are supposed to observe your mind to know exactly how your thoughts flow. Life is nothing but a movement of various attributes of energy in different frequencies for the consciousness to experience what living in duality is all about. Your mind is required to know who, what, and how you are spiritually, mentally, and physically. The self, being the observer, in the form of a soul is required to observe, check, guide, and use the mind, instead of being used by it.

Otherwise, the prejudiced mind keeps justifying, evaluating, and condemning everything with words and excuses from its own beliefs. The witness is that presence of your spirit, making your mind aware of its thoughts and feelings. The witness-er is that individual soul surfing in subjective awareness, disbanding separated thoughts and unifying them with self-awareness. It is that central contraption, which is not attached to anything—impersonal and impartial—your mind can extract through sheer witnessing.

- **Second Stage:** To be spiritual, adapt your mind to be continuously *alert and attentive*; allow it to become aware of all that is around, inside out. Watching and witnessing should be an effortless process, not requiring or engaging any desirous methods or practices. Mind, by default, develops alertness and is centred because it becomes focused and attentive, not making any efforts merely watching and witnessing all that is happening inside out. Now, instead of multitasking by habit, the same mind reaches a state of single-pointedness. Thoughts centralize from the constant chattering of past and future and become still as well as dynamic from one moment to another. Light up that inner awareness to explore the inner and the outer. You need to become aware of your self-ego and its relationship with the outside world.

- **Third Stage:** After awakening that spirit/soul in your body and mind, *neither identify nor attach* to your body and emotional mind. Be in it, yet not in it; be the centre of it, effortlessly and without making any choices. Allow the mind to freely undertake all its activity—with the soul/spirit watching attentively. It will make your mind aware and conscious of itself. Meditation means to be alert, still, and dynamic every moment. It means to be able to observe every thought and feeling and keep moving with it.

Meditation is a movement of the mind in silence without any conscious effort in the absence of a *meditator* . . . to be existentially aware of every moment in mindfulness. For instance, if you are reading this book attentively, absorbing every word, you are in meditation; the subject, which is you, becomes one with the object. Or when I am writing, if I am not alert and attentive, the outcome will be half-hearted and erratic. Meditation is not to control or suppress any thoughts but *to self-awaken your soul witnessing your thoughts in any present moment, centred with full alertness in total awareness.*

Only after understanding the above-mentioned stages, how to channelize and centralize your energy levels, you may consider your mind to have begun the journey of being spiritual. Soul as an observer is free from the mind's likes and dislikes. Because only after realizing this state, the mind and soul are independently in unity with each other. Unless you liberate yourself—those identifications and attachments from your cognitive mind—only after that, the personal me and mine will cease to exist. Liberation or moksha is nothing but becoming free from the mind and *all its desirous emotional thoughts,* which attach and identify to every object. When you no longer remain that seeker, seeking for enlightenment of any sort, the entrapped spirit becomes free from the mind. You, as the subject of life in the formless state of spirit, are merely a state of being-ness and not of any 'I, me, and self'.

This I-less or no-self state of being-ness is already enlightened and realized as the highest attribute of energy not requiring any further realization from the dual operating mind.

When the seeker, seeking the sought, becomes one without separation of any sort, your spirit becomes free from its field of consciousness. It is from this source, the core of who you are, awareness emerges, giving a meaning to your feelings and thoughts. Initially, thoughts are pure, spontaneous, choiceless, and total. Subsequently, consciousness takes over with the help of memory and intellect; the mind separates the oneness of every form of energy into its relative duality. This allows it to think, analyze, relate, choose, and experience between any two opposite factors, consciously or otherwise, for its self-interest from its past conditioning in beliefs.

I repeat, you as the formless spirit are a part of that universal divine energy, which has been imprisoned in the body and mind, labelled as spiritual awareness, entrapped in a soul symbolizing the witnessing self. Free this pure, potential energy from your mind, which is referred to as moksha. Come out of that shell of body and mind and taste the universe—the ocean of total awareness wherein there is nothing but bliss. It is beyond all your imaginations and conceptualizations. Universal awakening begins when meditation for your self-consciousness ends, making way for that selflessness in oneness, the way it was selflessly done by Mahatma Gandhi.

You are the presence of awareness confined to the body and mind. Please remember, you are not the process of any becoming; it is your mind (the thinking self) that needs to become something. You are already a finished product of total awareness confined in a soul—Thou Art That. Spirituality, humanity, divinity, etc., are all mental processes of becoming something to take the separated mind beyond illusions to understand the true nature of the self. There are no separate human gods in this game of life. Collective minds of any community identify with them like Krishna or Jesus due to their higher levels of consciousness to enforce morality through social effort and exertion in order to spread their message of virtuousness. As a result, what we eventually get is the birth of a religion. However, there is a lot of religiousness or oneness in religiosity; God and religion are meant to be a sublime flow of pure energy in higher consciousness to describe actions of humanity in humility in verbs rather than identifying them in nouns with names and genders for each separate religion.

Therefore, you are that potential divine spirit, and your spiritual role is meant just to watch and witness. Unfortunately, the material mind uses you and your consciousness and, in turn, remains ignorant about your true self. You are *not* the observer, but that *flow of observation*, which makes the mind responsible for observing the observed. The observer is that individualized soul, which later becomes that *thinker* after extending within the mind, whereas *you* are the presence of that spirit of aware energy trapped in a soul—Shivohum.

The thinking mind is merely a temporary exposition of materiality to engage in the dualities of life to experience both pleasure and pain. The cause of misery is the *thinking* mind with its bundle of fear, originating from the feelings of attachment to satiate material desires. The moment thoughts determine any sensation, desire arises; the mind identifies and attaches, chooses and separates the unity of any energy between this or that in duality. So, you need to be watchful of how to surf between the spiritual and the material with your third eye open to experience those dualities in life; the meaning and purpose of your physical existence. Or, be courageous enough to traverse towards that highest potential of your true self where you combine willpower and concentration as a priority, activity, and ultimate goal towards that divinity in self-awakening and self-transformation to realize bliss under all circumstances.

Fundamentally, there are two sensations—fear and love—out of which desire emerges. What exists is only love; in the absence of love, fear emanates, and to shield you from insecurity and fear, desire arises in multiple ways. In fear, the mind separates further becoming insecure, diverging from its source; in love, you converge. It is this self-awakening, which reveals boundless love hidden within your body and mind. The answer is already there—what you require is simply to understand your true self in order to witness all processes of the mind. Mindfully, meaning, centred by not swaying into past and future thoughts.

Be who you are —the enlightened spirit with your third eye (awareness) alert and open to watch and witness all that the mind does, which the mind (thinking self) wishes to experience in materiality with duality. The sense of separation, which the mind cultivates in duality, is an illusion. We, as well as all the other forms of energy, are indivisible even though all that exists is energy; it merely appears in interchangeable forms and goes back into its oneness. In dual living as male and female, abiding in dualities with relativity, we may separate temporarily, but ultimately, we are Advaita (not two).

You, as the spirit, are imprisoned in that mind of yours. Fear will take you through emotional desires with insecurity wanting something or the other for that tomorrow. Love, on the other hand, has that immense capacity to bypass the intellect and sneak into the depth of that ocean, which subsumes all that exists in universal love. It is that spiritual love beyond the selfish thinking self. The moment the mind becomes selfless, all bindings disappear, and you are set free . . . a flow of energy not requiring any explanation from the mind. The presence of my consciousness is within you, and that of yours is within me. It is that oneness where there is no me and you, no duality, the answer lies flowing in inclusiveness as one and not two.

As mentioned earlier, spirituality is the practice of the subject of spiritualism. It can only provide methods and processes to reform your mind to become something, which you, as the spirit, already are. If you can experience this silence in choiceless thoughts merely by watching and witnessing the body and mind, and neither be identified nor attached, your soul becomes free from all bindings. The mind then shifts from fear and insecurity towards love and solicitude, and in turn, you become the master of your mind. The unfolding of this true self is what we refer to as inner transformation.

Chapter 8

THE WITNESS

'Where the I is, the Infinite is not.
When the I ceases to be I, the Infinite shines in
all its glory.'
—Avadhuta Gita

THE SPIRIT IS TOTAL AWARENESS. SPIRITUALISM IS THE subject of the spirit and spirituality is a process of its study and practice by the mind to explore and discover the inner self (soul) to evolve and transform in that direction. You represent both—the physical form within a temporary thinking self in body-mind as well as that formless metaphysical self, the eternal spirit embodied in an individual soul. The mind is an operating system, which churns and processes data representing the same into action. During that processing, the thinking self, because of its constant desires, becomes more material than spiritual. When you consider yourself in ignorance to be that material self, the thinking self takes the body and mind on a roller-coaster ride of pleasure and pain.

However, when the mind is aware of the inner self, it awakens that infinite spiritual potentiality referred to as Thou Art That. When you know and understand who and what you are, the spiritual journey begins. Becoming something is only for the material self to experience and realize something unique—individuality. Humans like Jesus, Krishna, or Buddha transformed their uniqueness, realizing higher consciousness, and became eternal forever.

This something—which is assumed as physical, personal, or material in the form of body-mind—temporarily emerges and returns to its infinite abode in absoluteness, which you already are, embedded in the formless state of that intrinsic spirit composed within an individual soul. In such a permanent, unchanging reality, there is nothing to perceive, conceive, or realize. All transitory living forms merely present themselves to experience their uniqueness while they exist in physicality.

I repeat, during the becoming of your body and mind, the personal self remains temporary—changing, expanding, and evolving, say, like a cloud in the sky that comes and goes. Only because you, as that impersonal self, never change . . . remaining eternal as the sky. We can comfortably correlate the sky or the ocean with that spirit, which subsumes all that exists within its infinite presence. Eventually, there is no further experiencing or realizing to become something, but to remain as nothing in its infinitude of absolute emptiness known as Shunyata.

Once you know, understand, and experience you are the spirit, the sky, or the ocean, you awaken simply to *witness* all desires manifesting in the mind, becoming free from all identifications and attachments, which limit the mind. You understand your true presence as the spirit and lucidly watch and witness all that is happening. Seeking for this self-knowledge begins with a desire to a point where you make all efforts to evolve from the lower towards the higher consciousness with all those methods provided by spirituality. When you finally become aware that you are none other than what you are seeking, the seeker seeking the sought becomes one. All seeking ends, and you merely remain as an observer watching blissfully all that the mind perceives and conceives in consciousness.

There is nothing wrong with motivational efforts to discipline and practise to go beyond—from the lower to that higher consciousness—in material self. In such a transformed *becoming*, the transient body and mind mature to realize you are already 'That Thou Art'. Since you—as that individualized spirit—are imprisoned in mind, *becoming* initiates a disciplined approach to free your soul from that cage called mind, allowing it to merge with selfless love towards that universal oneness dispassionately. The continuity in unity created by such dispassionate love remains eternal and brings you towards the centre of that space of nothing—the infinite expanse of pure potential awareness. This was very well exemplified to the world by Mahatma Gandhi during his extraordinary journey of *satyagraha* (non-violent resistance) while fighting a war, without firing a single bullet.

Awareness transforms thoughts, and thoughts, in turn, affect the flow of energy. Since all ideas as well feelings—material or spiritual—originate from the mind, an enlightened person is the one who can live as a witness not bound to the mind, yet *acting* through the mind. He or she performs every worldly act, and despite that remains unaffected and uninvolved by the desires and emotions of the mind in the role of a witness.

Please keep in mind, during a state of witnessing, there is no doing; the mind is that doer, which you cannot deny. To become a witness, you just need to become free from the mind from its identifications and attachments, the cause for all insecurities. If attached to the mind, the ego is essential; if not, you become a witness. I repeat, one who has attained the state of being a constant witness is fully aware and not bound to anything. He or she is *in mind* but does not belong to the mind.

Non-attached action happens on its own, without any desire. Moreover, for any feeling, thought, or action, the mind depends upon consciousness (what you are), which, in turn, depends upon the source (awareness—who you are). The mind is merely a mechanical operating system of who and what you are. The source (creator) plainly witnesses, and the consciousness initiates that creation through the mind, depending on what you have become from the personal intensity (intelligence) in the usage of your source, i.e., awareness.

Consciousness is for the material world. The spirit remains passive as nothing. It is that creator, which is not aware of its creation but can make the mind aware to materialize creation. There can be no change in your spirit as it has zero becoming. The individualized soul is that witness-er, which we refer to as the witnessing consciousness that merely incorporates total awareness.

Meaning, you, as the spirit, in total awareness remain eternal and do not change. You neither incarnate nor reincarnate. Hence, you do not alter or *become*—you only observe through the soul, that is, if awakened to make the mind aware and conscious, which, in turn, effortlessly transforms your body and mind without the real you even becoming aware of its presence. It is only the mind that becomes something out of its state of consciousness in order to create its individuality or uniqueness, which is the meaning and purpose of your individual life.

Again, you, as the spirit, do not require to become spiritual; it is mind that needs to evolve and transform. Do not make any attempts to change. Any change by your mind is for the material purpose, and you—being the spirit—always remain changeless. Change is imperative for the mind to become something within its play of cause and effect. Do not make any effort from the mind to become spiritual because the more effort you make, it will rebound stronger with extra vigour, which we refer to as ego. For the mind, a different kind of adjustment is required— the *growth* of your consciousness towards the higher self (soul) when you disidentify from thoughts, solely through awareness. I agree it is natural to change, but not for the soul. Change is for the material mind to expand, experience, effectuate, and evolve in duality for the enlargement of ego-consciousness or transform into higher consciousness.

The spiritual seeker understands that all changes are transitory. It depends upon how well you know this world materially or spiritually. What you need to keep in mind is not to get confused between the meanings behind the word spirit and soul; the subject of spiritualism and in its practice of spirituality. The latter indicates the direction towards the subject—spirit. As mentioned earlier, the soul, meaning, the witnessing consciousness, requires no disciplining, training, transcending, or transforming. Spirituality is that mental and physical reformative process of concentrating, conditioning, and coaching out of motivation in various methods and techniques administering the mind towards the direction of the soul. It brings you to the outer edge of that centre, and after that your soul—directly in link with the spirit—takes over witnessing between the material and the spiritual to celebrate what we call life.

Let us summarize again on our understanding of the meaning and definition of the term spirit, spirituality, and being spiritual. I repeat, in spirituality, your mind is provided with mental techniques to acquire skills to superintend the mind. To be spiritual, you merely need to witness that material self and make the mind aware and conscious of surrendering the mind to accept all that exists in its sensitivity of oneness. It is that spirit, the divine within, which, in no manner, requires any experience of vagaries in life. All it does is observe and witness the mind through the soul, making it aware and conscious to experience and realize based on its level of consciousness.

The mind is a restless operator flowing through random thoughts, always in flux. It requires the spirit to counter this restlessness in order to make it aware and conscious of all that is . . . in and out. Otherwise, thoughts remain chaotic and insecure under the influence of desires and fear. Desire is that fuel, which drives the mind, creating a sensation to feel for something. Feelings, in turn, provide ideas, imagination, and fantasies resulting in thoughts of beliefs . . . conditioning the brain into a rigid and biased product. You experience what you believe, continuously fearing for its outcome: 'Is it going to be favourable or not?' This, in turn, leads to insecurity, anxiety, misery, and suffering. Even if you manage to control or suppress the mind temporarily, the desire within remains— whether it is for the material or spiritual. It is that source or spirit seated within the brain, which opposes this random nature of the mind in sublimity. Unfortunately, very few are aware of the role of the spirit because of which we suffer from so much anxiety and depression.

For instance, you regularly and consistently watch and witness your emotional thoughts revolving around your past and future. In that case, the mind becomes aware and gradually weans away from becoming unconsciously dependent on your thoughts. The mind relaxes, takes it easy, and becomes focused in the present moment. It is now alert and aware, and the spirit from that superconscious section of the mind indirectly and effortlessly guides your mind in sheer observation without any interference from your thoughts. The mind shifts from the material towards a spiritual tangent. It is no longer concerned about any gain or loss, but it intelligibly flows, spontaneously and proactively acting on what it wishes.

Therefore, it may not be necessary for you to use various methods of spirituality to disconnect from anything that your mind may consider unfavourable. It is difficult to detach after becoming attached because the mind will not permit any suppression. In fact, it will redouble with extra strength. What you require is effortless monitoring through sheer witnessing of your thoughts. The mind becomes shy of being watched and withdraws after becoming aware, resulting in becoming conscious of what it is about to experience. Ideas are the origin of the brain. They become much more accessible through witnessing if you can arrest the unfavourable ones right at the beginning, otherwise, the mind turns them progressively into habits, and detaching from them later is a tedious process.

Thus, what is required is to fool this phenomenal mind, which subconsciously and anxiously runs in an autopilot mode. Not by methods of suppression or trying to control the brain, but by becoming aware and conscious from that witnessing spirit. Most approaches to control the mind with various techniques given by spirituality go in vain because they do *not* stress upon that inner witness-er to awaken the spirit and be vigilant. Gradually, practices like yoga, meditation, etc., also become mechanical, autonomous, and even unconscious after some time. The mind then bounces back to its original egoist self with the subconscious level taking over the reins. You are back into the rut from where you started. We remain engrossed in self-identity with self-attachments within the sphere of our self-interest.

Therefore, more than applying methods to discipline the mind through mantras, meditation, or mindfulness, quietly watch the mind, and it will become conscious of its movements. The moment you *watch* your mind, it becomes aware and alert. It starts to behave itself and awakens to what it is experiencing. It is so similar to, say, if someone is staring at you, your mind becomes wary and cautious of what it is about to do, or of its doing.

If you stress on the practice of spiritual methods, they become routine and habitual, resulting primarily in boosting your ego. You can see this clearly in most spiritual artists who are always seeking attention from the media and elsewhere, impressing upon others for the sake of applause and to increase their followers in return. Furthermore, after those mental exercises are over, you are back to square one; remaining the same egoist, bragging about your practice to others, seeking appreciation and recognition in some form or another. We are all the same; you certainly cannot consider *that* being spiritual!

So, the mind is either tilted towards materiality or in the direction of its true self. In the case of the latter, there are certain traits that are familiar to those who follow either by default or with intention:

- The mind is continuously alert, attentive, and focused
- They are sensitive to all as one and not sentimental towards a few of their near and dear ones
- Surrender and accept all situations and circumstances; neither being excited or agitated with grace and respect, irrespective of success or failure, happiness or sadness
- Share their wealth and knowledge with others and are spontaneously generous
- Do not exhibit their ego and share credit with all
- Are aware of the fact that they are above body and mind
- Know the meaning of and difference between spiritualism, spirituality, spiritual, and the spirit in the subject of life
- Surrender their mind in favour of the spirit, knowing they are spiritual beings going through a human experience
- Last, but most important, they continuously *watch and witness* their mind in its flow of thoughts, i.e., they are spiritually conscious

Chapter 9

UNDERSTANDING THE NATURE OF THE HUMAN MIND

*'Burn down the forest of ignorance with the fire
of the understanding that
"I am the one pure awareness," and be happy
and free from distress.'*
—John Richards, Ashtavakra Gita (1.9)

An EXPERIENTIALLY REALIZED AND TRANSFORMED MIND is expected to be conscious, calm, and caring—functioning in the here and now, experiencing to realize harmony with other minds. However, in actuality, it is different. Pleasantness in humans is confined to its nature of thinking, feeling, desiring, condemning, justifying, imitating, and clinging to self-identification and attachments . . . fundamentally seeking pleasure and avoiding pain. This sort of nature occurs because the mind selfishly wishes for one single implementation—a delight of any sort. It subconsciously focuses in an unconscious manner, motivated towards desires, where efforts are directed on how to derive continuous comfort and gratification solely for that *me and mine*, least sensitive to what is happening around.

Desire is that fuel and source of mind's power. Like any other mechanical system, the energy of the mind also requires another form of energy or stimulation to start and sustain its performance, which in our case is desire. From wanting to live, eat, drink, and sleep, all material and spiritual functions connect to desire. Not to desire is also a form of desire. It activates the subconscious to continue moving in its flow of thoughts and, after that, into an autonomous mode in unconscious actions. A subconscious mind is that thinking self, acquiring data from its memory and intellect, not requiring any conscious effort. Thus, a thinker is more of a formation of combined thoughts, analyzing and resolving all material decisions, identified and attached primarily for its desire to expand and accumulate this and that. It is for this reason you never say, 'I am thoughts' but refer to the same as *your* thoughts.

So, what is desire? It is more of an emotion, a feeling originating from an idea. The mind enters into a field of imagination, fantasizing that idea into a belief convincing the mind: 'This is what I want and shall experience.' Please remember, all these happenings that occur are mechanical in an auto mode, without the mind being fully aware and conscious of such thoughts. In self-interest, thoughts surrounding such attractions revolve around the past projecting the same into the future—since desire is always something for the future.

Unconsciously, you fantasize about its outcome and imagine the pleasures you will relish from its realization. It is similar to the motion of a pendulum swinging from one end to another. The mind bypasses the present situated at its centre, evaluating from its past thoughts for its future wants. Therefore, even though all impulses, sensations, and feelings capture desire in the present moment, however, before arriving at an answer, the mind mulls upon past data for its desired effect in the future. It emotionally decides based on self-interest, discriminates and determines the data available from the past to act and infer to please itself. All this activity occurs in an auto mode, without the mind feeling the need to be conscious about what is happening in the thinking self.

In such a manner, the mind responds to any situation or stimulus unconsciously, reacting only to what it feels, thinks, and acts. Instead of immediately being aware of the present moment, it takes time to separate the non-dual impulses of observation into its dual thinking, relating, and analyzing one factor from another in opposites. Subconsciously, the mind ponders upon its effect for its self-interest, and unconsciously experiences more from its memory and intellect. Meaning, prior knowledge combined with biased reasoning rather than with the totality of any situation at hand in the present moment. Therefore, the mind is that doer doing through the mind, the object in question.

Thoughts always connect to the past because it takes time to think while the present passes by. Thoughts are dependent and relate to memory because they are attuned to react out of want and emotions. The spirit, on the other hand, is that presence of you—the being-ness spontaneously observes and pro-acts in the now. Being is merely that quantitative factor of your existence consisting of body and mind. It is that being-ness, the essence, the spirit, and the soul, which determines that quality, state, or condition of your true self at any given time of your bodily existence.

After perceiving through its senses, the mind subconsciously evaluates from its memory, analyzes for its future through its intellect to experience what it desires, evading the present. Spirituality demands all three to combine as one in totality for its fulfilment in all respects. It is not the division of time but the spontaneous moment of any duration from one moment to the next that matters. Therefore, all three—the past, present, and future—impressions of intellectual information from the past, intelligence, and intuition in the present moment, and instinct for its future combine as one. Only if we are alert, aware, and attentive existentially from moment to moment in order to pro-act and not react to any situation consciously.

Always keep in mind, the past was once the present; the future is the present yet to come; and the now is that eternal present moment, as it is, the way it is, existing in that is-ness at any particular moment. It is the mind, which separates the holistic nature of now into three dimensions. The past and future originate from the thinking self, whereas the present is the domain of the spiritual self when thoughts are absent and you enter into your qualitative self.

For this reason, meditative awareness is an essential tool where you silence your thoughts for a while to discipline the mind to go towards that centre, the spirit. Learn how to still the mind through silence, solitude, and serenity to be able to effortlessly flow in meditative awareness, attentively watching every present moment the way it is, without any concern for the past or future. Spirituality provides methods to tame the mind from oscillating between the past and the future. If awakened, the spirit urges the cognitive mind to spontaneously act from its superconscious section instead of considering and calculating every reaction subconsciously.

Therefore, the cognitive or the material mind limits us. Since the mind functions over 95 per cent from its subconscious levels in an auto mode from its memory and intellect, it is restricted to the past and future. We remain limited to other's knowledge believing and following this and that of what we read and hear from multiple sources. Our intellect carries excess baggage of the outdated, exhausting knowledge. It is the present, which is exclusively ours, intuitively and instinctively providing our mind with the fresh creative intelligence of the now to self-create our uniqueness. When all three—past, present, and future—combine, the human mind becomes infinite and limitless.

If we permit the cognitive mind to act on its own, mainly from the memory and its intellect, it remains unconsciously inclined towards anxiety and insecurity. Why? Because we usually are concerned more about the future rather than the task at hand. However, suppose we are alert and attentive in the present moment, the spirit awakens to observe any situation, making the mind aware and, after that, conscious about what it is going to perform. The past, present, and future only divide the now into a time-measured factor; otherwise, all three support, nourish, and validate the significance of any moment for its fulfilment in totality.

Furthermore, the mind cannot survive without faith and belief, which are also dependent on the past. Hopes are based on desires concerning the future responsible for creating fear of the unknown. You continuously remain uncertain and the crucial present moment silently passes by. If you are alert, the mind is in the present, the spirit awakens to assist you all the way because you are now centred, dynamic, and focused in the now . . . not bothering about the past or its future results. Both anxiety and fear vanish because you are proactive. Moreover, you are spontaneous, without giving any time for the mind to think into this or that, here and there.

The mind's activity has been divided by time so that the past, present, and future can respectively be measured in accordance with their completion in any material realization. What we need is to discipline the mind to chatter less, either in the past or future, so that we can concentrate better in the present and that, too, consciously.

The spirit, on the other hand, as mentioned earlier, does not require any experiencing or evolving. It is the mind that remains ignorant of its true self or the soul. It unconsciously chatters and mostly remains imbalanced, substantially and materially tilted towards the outer world. Consequently, there exists disorder and disparity in most families, society, community, and country, irrespective of whatever methods of psychology, philosophy, or spirituality they may profess or follow. Until and unless the spirit observes and witnesses the direction the mind is moving towards or how one feels, thinks, and acts every moment, it is not possible to understand any situation in its proper perspective.

You will agree if there is ample dissatisfaction, arrogance, and unhappiness, whether among the rich or poor, there must be something drastically wrong in the manner we exist and conduct ourselves on this earth. All of us are concerned about following some method or effort provided by gurus and mahatmas ranting and chanting on what was told during prehistoric times, subjugated under superstitions and supernatural theories. All they do is cultivate your mind in outdated beliefs, ideologies, and imaginations. Thus, we keep changing from one guru to another in search of following something or the other. For instance, we can continuously watch and witness our thoughts, not being rigid and conditioned, not condemning and justifying, open and free in silence. Your mind becomes composed and calm, which is not a development of the mind but of that spirit ushering creativity in total awareness.

Don't we have enough evidence of the chaos, killings, and disturbances prevalent all around? As you read, the majority of the world is reeling under misery, poverty, and suffering; creatures big or small are living in pain and fear, the earth is being looted so that a few humans may continue to use them for pleasure and profit. How rampantly we are destroying the world that provides us with everything. And this is happening because, for generations, we are conditioned to remain ignorant about the nature of our actual reality and that of the world.

The ones who are supposed to be leaders and preachers are but marketeers of their personal philosophy. If we wish to improve this world and our relationship with all that exists, first, we need to understand ourselves and stop following anything or anyone blindly. The subject of spiritualism elaborates on the context and content of life. Please consider it seriously as a seeker, independently, and not out of depression or anxiety. Do not go too much after methods, techniques, and efforts that will invite artists, celebrities, and authorities who provide temporary solace from your misery and anxiety. I suppose, for that, you will require a psychiatrist more than a guru.

Self-knowledge is all-important and of significant consequence. If we do not know and understand who and what we are, we have no authority or liberty over our thoughts that belong to us. What other options do we have besides knowing and understanding this subject called spiritualism? We need to understand it without the interference of science or religion because religion, today, separates one from another, and science is never sure about what it declares. Both try to prove their superiority over this philosophy because we remain ignorant and do not bother to know of our inner formless self. We must study, learn, understand, and experience this subject independently, free from any affiliation or amalgamation. Only then we will be able to capture the true essence of spiritualism, which declares that fear is your biggest enemy and love is your most generous friend.

Self-knowledge can come only from understanding this subject in its true essence and cannot be provided from any outside source. Authorities and books can only show you the direction, the rest is for you to understand and realize. It is your alert mind that can make your mind aware and free from blind beliefs, imaginations, and ideologies. You are not what others are trying to convince. I reiterate, you are that potential divine, the ultimate intelligence, which needs to be awakened . . . not by efforts or methods but by being alert, attentive, aware, and conscious.

Moreover, the underlying problem with the mind is that it avoids and hides from the truth. It relies more on relative truth, which differs from one to another. Furthermore, the personal thinking self is designed by the mind to think narrowly for its selfish desires where reality, truth, and self-development are dictated more by parents, teachers, society, community, and politicians belonging to any and every country. They imprison the mind with blind beliefs, fear, and violence where we become dependent on others following them without even bothering to explore the truth.

Thus, a human mind—prejudiced, conditioned, and rigid—remains predisposed with preconceived ideas, losing its freedom. Hence, most of us are least concerned about truth, reality, the role of the spirit, or what spiritual awareness is all about. We have no patience to understand the subject seriously. We rely upon and bargain more for myths and mysticism where mythological thrillers and supernatural fables containing spicy, seductive, and sensual titles allure us, which are far more in demand than literary books like the one you are reading.

Therefore, please do not get influenced by any authority— be it God, atman, religious tenets, and spiritual artists. If you do, belief emerges, turning into faith. As a result, your freedom of thought depletes, you become limited to feelings of beliefs that further promote insecurity and fear. The mind gets biased, not caring for reason and clarity. Hence, learn from all authoritative sources, listen to their messages— which they wish to convey—but do not bind your mind, limiting its potentiality. The human brain is the source of infinite potentiality; it requires freedom from all beliefs and bindings, whatsoever, to flow freely in order to explore, experience, evolve, and effectuate to realize all dualities of life with zero attachments and identifications to become one with the soul.

Please keep in mind that the spirit is always free, enlightened, realized, and aware. It requires no further transcendence. It is that transcendent, the potential divine, residing within every one of us and the reason for declaring 'Thou Art That'. We should free ourselves from this mental cage bound to identifications and attachments and lucidly know that we are the spirit. Only then will the soul be able to witness freely what our thoughts feel and desire and whether they enact righteously or not, which, in turn, assists the conscious and the subconscious sections of the mind.

Therefore, life is a culmination of personal experiences with their respective realizations. It incorporates the totality of past, present, and future from one moment to the next in any situation. What the mind establishes at any given moment is an amalgamation of memories of the past, awareness of the present, and desires for the future. Life reveals and reflects through your body and mind, what you were in the past, what you are now, and what you desire to become in the future. It is a consummation of your physical and mental expansion, evolving in the present, longing to progress and transform in every future moment. Hence, please do not negate the past, present, or future as they all need to unite to complete and fulfil a certain level of uniqueness, which you are meant to create in this life.

It is that totality, the ultimate substrata, which reflects the accurate picture of life in its timeless realm as one and not two. Truth, reality, love, God, etc., all these factors belong to that existential moment, which is changeless, existing as it is, the way it is in the eternal now. For example, I perceive a cup in my hand as real and authentic so long as the shape is intact, the way it is, as it is in the now for the period that it lasts. Say, the moment it falls and smashes into pieces, a different perception or truth emerges for that new moment of now. The mind dissects the duration of any present moment into the past, present, and future—measuring, evaluating, and relating what it perceives for its convenience—creating differences of that change or relative truth in illusions. Therefore, let us go further in order to understand the absolute truth from its relative aspect.

Absolute is that all-pervasive; encompassing everything that exists. Meaning, the entire universe is a self-manifestation of the only absolute awareness from which all diversities emanate. Spiritually as well as scientifically, everything at its fundamental level is what we refer to as spirit or energy. There is no such thing as physical reality. Whatever appears to the brain as physical is a probability wave in its subatomic realm flowing in unity and continuity as one. Moreover, for anything to appear as visible or tangible, there has to be someone to observe in the first place. It is that highest attribute of the spirit, which is causeless and is beyond space and time. The same has been accredited by our ancient sages to be the ultimate reality in the form of absolute awareness. The divine essence of all perception, which unfolds everything to light in order to experience the dualities of life.

To clarify further, we take the same example as above: When I observe the cup from my sense organs, it merely means I am *aware* of the cup, as it is, the way it is, in that moment of now. Later, when the cup is broken, again, I am *aware* that the cup is now damaged from my new observation. 'Awareness' is always there because observation here is common and present in both cases, whereas the cup is not, nor is its broken parts. If we further break this down to its tiniest subatomic level, all we have is condensed energy vibrating in a specific frequency that can change into waves of the quantum field the moment the flow of observation moves.

Therefore, the knowledge behind all this happening is observation, which comprises what we are *aware* of. Meaning, the essence behind all knowledge is nothing but its ultimate reality in the form of the spirit: *The presence of eternal awareness in waves of potential energy revealing itself in possibilities of matter and consciousness.* Please remember, *lifeless matter* is not aware. Knowing is that quality of awareness or that understanding, which expresses itself through its wakefulness from consciousness in life.

The present is timeless because its duration can extend to any period. The sky is eternal, whereas the clouds are not. The past and future are hypothetically placed by the mind, before and after the present moment to analyze, measure, and infer mathematically. Prima facie, time is always ticking, it is going and gone . . . what permanently exists is only the present. The past was once the present, the present is the present, and the future is yet to become the present. Therefore, the present is absolute, without any beginning or end, existing independently, not requiring any support. The world in which we live is relative; it requires the provision of its opposite— past relating to its future to sustain itself.

Moreover, if you wish to know what actual reality is, you

should be more concerned with its essence; the knowledge of what ultimate truth is in the eternal now. The fundamental absolute reality is one without a second, the only reality from which all forms manifest. The absolute, which is devoid of all diversities, yet all diversities emanate from its absoluteness. Both are real—the transient matter as well as the eternal spirit. All transitory forms are subsumed under the substratum of the, one and only, absolute awareness on which everything that temporarily exists is superimposed. There is no such thing as unreal since all that exists in this universe is not two; hence, the unreal is just a metaphor. The ultimate reality is the ground of all being, which is beyond science because physics is more concerned with physicality, which is observable and measured. In contrast, the ultimate reality is beyond all conceptions formulated by the human mind.

In this manner, thoughts always relate to the past, awareness will be of now, and you hope for that tomorrow that is yet to come. All relativities are but extensions of the absolute separating to their extreme ends. Without the memories of the past, you will not know your name, gender, or even who and what you are. Nor is your mind able to recapitulate how your experiences of today reflect upon past actions, resulting in the formation of today to further create its tomorrow. I repeat, all three are nothing but extensions of that one and only, the present.

I reiterate, the mind keeps brooding and boasting about its past, fantasizing about its future. It is primarily for this reason, you, as the spirit, are required to continually witness in order to be aware of your mind through the presence of your spirit. Stay connected mainly with the essence of every knowledge. The superconscious section captures the now and the conscious stage utilizes the now to evolve. In contrast, the subconscious plays the drama of life unconsciously in illusions, bypassing the presence of any present moment. All three combine to create that totality of fulfilment, something we desire. Hence, the mind provides the necessary data from its past and future thoughts, and the spirit, while spontaneously witnessing with choiceless thoughts, makes the mind aware and conscious of the present moment.

Chapter 10

YOU ARE THAT ULTIMATE REALITY

*'There are no divine scriptures, no world, no
imperative religious practices;
There are no gods, no classes or races of men,
No stages of life, no superior or inferior;
There's nothing but Brahman, the supreme
Reality.'*
—S. Abhayananda, The Avadhuta Gita

*I*N THE SUBJECT OF LIFE, WE HAVE TWO PERSPECTIVES—
the physical and the spiritual. The former manifests as mortal
and is temporary, the latter is fundamental and eternal. The
body and mind are taken as transitory, while the spirit is
that ultimate. All three—body, mind, and spirit—combine to
provide a special life to every living creature; a story, which
is unique to each in order to taste and experience what life
is all about. So, the ultimate reality is that screen on which
everything appears and disappears, on which the whole drama
of life is played. The movie finishes and vanishes; the body and
mind, as actors, disappear. You, as that state of being-ness (the
spirit of total awareness) within a soul, remain as the ultimate
reality. It is that unchanging screen of understanding, which
is our true identity—the witness of all perceptions in thoughts
and appearances.

Now, what is this ultimate reality? The paragraph above indicates that all manifestations are from the same reality, one without a second—the spirit, which is beyond the mind, soul, and its experiences. Quantum physics refers to that as energy, while spiritualism says it is Brahman, the highest attribute of which has been set down as awareness. It has this distinctive quality of ultimacy; it is singular and free from all conceptualizations. We have the ultimate reality presenting itself as the absolute quintessence of all things. Spiritualism considers this absolute nature of the spirit to be in total awareness since everything that exists has ever existed or will exist later, occurring entirely because of *awareness*.

Awareness is the *essence of all perceptions* because you can perceive something only after you become aware of it. It is that primordial foundation and fountainhead—the creator of all creations. The highest attribute of this ultimate reality, if and when fully awakened, has also been ascribed as Paramatma, *Parmeshwar*, etc. The presence of awareness reveals itself passively (not being aware of its own self) within the human mind, waiting to be evoked in its highest capacity as that noumenal from which the phenomenal human mind is associated and identified. You being that presence with that intensity of individual awareness (being-ness) in every individual mind become identical to that noumenal creator silently residing within its own creation: 'Thou Art That'. Those who endorse and assert this supreme energy are considered to be nontheistic, and the ones who separate the creator from its creation to believe in personal human gods become religious in a theistic manner.

Figuring out what is real is another complicated issue. What we observe, see, believe, comprehend, measure, or become aware of are different connotations to define reality. So, reality, by perception, does not mean it is really real as stated in quantum physics. It is more of a possibility in potentialities rather than being actual. Thus, the debate over the nature of reality is highly confusing because Einstein once commented by saying, 'Reality is merely an illusion, albeit a very persistent one.' The nearest science has approached to anything being real is until someone observes, which is also not a complete answer to that unchanging ultimate reality.

The subject of spiritualism as we all know is philosophical and not accountable to prove any of its dictums; that is the job of science. Therefore, in metaphysics, the ultimate reality is that I-less state of our being-ness, which is changeless—one without a second, spaceless, timeless, ultimate, and eternal. It is that absolute state of being-ness in total awareness, the one behind many when there is nothing left to observe and witness—a state of non-being in totality in which there is no such thing as a 'self'. It is that divine within where everything becomes known.

Being-ness is that rhapsody about the all-encompassing nature of the absolute ultimate reality, beyond everything that cognition can grasp. It is that state, which is constant and that which is always there, beyond space and time and cause and effect, since awareness precedes that which is around us. The universe unfolds in that awareness. Therefore, the ultimate reality is that absolute energy in total awareness—complete and indivisible—that which can neither be created nor destroyed, and is the substratum of all that temporarily exists in the universe.

The spirit comprises waves of formless energy—the eternal absolute from which an aware force emerges radiating its field, which we refer to as consciousness. Awareness is that noumenal, which provides that knowingness through phenomenal attributes diverging from its centeredness, perceiving a variety of new forms. These subset forms indicate a mid-reality during the period they exist in the form of subatomic particles of energy colliding, condensing, and combining in different frequencies as building blocks of atoms and molecules. In the form of matter incarnating as gross energy, superimposed on the ultimate presence of its absolute. It is only after the observer, observing through the mind, observes these objective forms that they seem to appear as real. Names and descriptions are stipulated, and when they disintegrate into their substrate, all these names and forms disappear into that oneness from where they had emerged.

Thus, the spirit residing within the human brain is considered to be the presence of that ultimate existence, temporarily individualizing and symbolizing itself as the witnessing self (soul) . . . the force within, which makes the body/mind awake, active, and alive through its field of consciousness. Wakefulness of any individual today is beyond scientific apprehension. Being metaphysical, we refer to that as the awakening spirit entrapped within the mind. I reiterate, when this universal spirit of awareness gets contained in an individual human mind, we refer to that as the soul. It is that impersonal and impartial higher component of human nature signifying the witnessing consciousness in contrast to the lower representing as the ego-consciousness, which is the total wakefulness of a human mind.

The soul is that inert, absolute aware energy, which is responsible for making the mind awake, aware, and conscious, while remaining passive, watching and witnessing what the cognitive mind experiences. It is that potential divine, which, if awakened, has infinite abilities to make the mind spontaneously aware towards boundless discoveries. Otherwise, the mind continuously—by default—functions in auto mode, unconsciously, from its subconscious section that is primarily for its material self in ego-consciousness.

The universe is a state of pure potentiality existing in the emptiness of an infinite space consisting of nothing but waves of dormant aware energy as the only existence. Therefore, when we presume any sort of existence as a 'thing', it is an illusory phenomenon cropping up temporarily from its noumenal to go back into the same. Since the noumenal represents nothing and from this nothingness transient phenomenal attributes keep appearing and disappearing, we can safely conclude that nothing is everything and everything is nothing.

The absolute passive energy is continuously expressing itself in a subset of interchangeable energies from its creation, destruction, and recreation, expanding and evolving only to eventually go back into its absoluteness. That something, though transient, is everything for us . . . observable and comprehensible, a mid-reality, the nature of which we conceptualize as our world consisting of matter and consciousness. Both the temporary and the permanent existences are real because the former comes out of the latter and goes back into the same, indicating all that exists is one and not two since the unreal cannot exist.

Almost all subjects, including science, base our understanding on this temporary mid-reality. We confine our thoughts predominantly to physicality, from personal gods to body and brain, and their relation to society, community, religion, country, and this world. However, there are a few who go beyond into the spiritual realm and comprehend that they are more than the body and mind. They understand that there is an aware, conscious principle beyond both the body and brain, something that identifies humans as the ultimate, which means that both the ultimate (spirit) and the illusory manifest as one composite unit—body, mind, and spirit.

This truth reveals a certain presence of awareness, which makes a human mind comprehend the concept of an imperishable ultimate reality. It also indicates the concept of mid-reality in the human forms of body-mind, representing that temporary thinking self. I repeat, it is this philosophical foundation of ultimate reality, the spirit of total awareness, which makes the body-mind aware and conscious of everything to become something that is unique to each one of us while we are alive.

Those who understand that we are more than the body and mind look beyond this limited vision entering into the mysterious spiritual realm of awareness and consciousness. Spiritualism is the study of this remarkable concept of self-knowledge, and spiritual awareness is the most consequential term used in its elucidation. Thus, please keep in mind, awareness prevails before (dormant) and also after (awakened) for everything we observe. The whole universe unfolds merely because of this aware observation by the human mind.

The world today is materially aware but not spiritually. We have made tremendous progress in science and technology but significantly lag in spiritual insight. This imbalance has created chaos and unrest all over the world, and we do not know how to address this precarious situation. Spiritual awareness in no manner indicates connecting with the divine; it primarily connects the ultimate nature to the physical self as one and not two. It activates the mind to observe itself in the present moment so that you may begin to realize less as an individual and more as a part of the universe as a whole. It is that presence of immediate aware energy, which is not attached to cognition. It is meant to spontaneously witness inwards in order to explore and discover our physical self, to observe our thoughts without any consent, condemnation, or justification. It is that aware ingredient, which is responsible for making us conscious.

After we can differentiate between the unconscious and the conscious, we awaken that true dormant self, which makes us superior to other animals. Otherwise, we mechanically remain a construct of space and time—physical, psychological, and chronological—living in the past through memory. In such a case, memory and intellect take over in an auto mode, subconsciously and quantitatively providing recognition of our physical identification to attachments from the past projecting additional desires into the future. Inversely, awareness is that quality of being awake to any present moment. In self-witnessing, we come to know the true nature of the mind and the role that it plays. We then begin to see the actual presence of 'who we are'—the inner secret of the brain. Furthermore, for the mind to create an inert relationship with this spirit, all one needs is to be effortlessly alert, attentive, and aware.

Spiritually, the most incredible illusion in a person's life is that he or she thinks that they are awake, whereas they are not. Meaning, our mind, at any given time in any situation, is in a state of continuous sleep, thinking only of the past and future rather than being in the present. The cognitive mind can never be in the present moment because it operates subconsciously in an autopilot mode from its subconscious level. Thus, it is considered to be spiritually asleep even when awake.

In spiritual terms, the mind is awake only when it is aware and conscious, knowing, and understanding *what* it is consciously experiencing in any present moment. Consciousness is considered to be that quantity of 'what' you are, and the presence of awareness forms the quality of 'who' you are. Life is but a combination of experiencing the dualities of life in relativity to know and understand the transcendental level of who and what we are—the subject of spiritualism refers to this as self-knowledge. Vedanta claims the same understanding to be the end of all knowledge, clarifying that when knowledge reaches its pinnacle, truth emerges.

The illusions arise because of the mind's difficulty in understanding the following salient features of spiritualism:

1. I am the presence of an abstract, formless ingredient of the universe, occurring in individual waves of aware potential energy called the spirit, which is responsible for making the mind of all living creatures awake and alive. Humans have the highest intensity of this conscious energy and are thus designated—Aham Brahmasmi, you are that spiritual aware conscious energy.

2. A human mind remains distorted—even when the body and brain are active—unless it is aware and conscious.

3. The nature of reality has two aspects—one is within the volume (space and time) in causation, and the

other is beyond cause and effect, space and time. Awareness is subjective, which creates possibilities through its field of consciousness, the ground of all objective beings. 'I Am' is only an illusory movement of thought in consciousness—a construct of mind in duality. In quantum physics, outside of space and time, we have only waves of energy, but after the mind observes in consciousness within space and time, they appear as particles. Hence, the brain is a phenomenon of consciousness, and awareness is that noumenal of all phenomena.

4. In quantum creativity, when energy vibrates, this reverberation makes it move. In motion, every living form of energy expands and evolves, expressing its being-ness (awakeness), exhibiting something unique from its field of becoming-ness, which is also concomitantly responsible for making the human mind conscious, awake, and alive with the highest potentiality. Thus, perception, memory, intellect, and consciousness, all combine and coordinate with each other when waves of energy collapse into particles, clarifying that the subject of awareness (qualified energy) activates only after the mind observes, to become aware and conscious of what it perceives. However, awareness is before and after all activities of the mind.

5. Awareness is that ignition to life, which awakens the soul to evolve and transform the mind into higher consciousness.

6. The absolute dark matter and energy (unqualified and unadulterated) always remains constant and complete. It is indivisible and from this wholesomeness. All the other forms of energies emerge and go back into the same, signifying that the Creator and its creations are the same. All that exists is not two, i.e., it is Advaita.

7. The wave of energy in any given object or event collapses into particles of actuality only when an observer looks at it. Observation is the primary subject of living to know the nature of reality—outer as well as inner. Only then the unknown becomes known. This is how the universe unfolds in the presence of our awareness, where everything that is, that was, and that will be exists only after the mind is aware through the observatory power of the brain. Without observation, no manifestation can be measured or verified.

Now, why do these illusions arise in the mind?

Firstly, because of the delusion created through space and time, observation takes place in the presence of now in choiceless thoughts, without any constraints from space and time or with cause and effect. It is total, non-dual, and absolute. Whereas, overall perception occurs in a specified space that requires time to move in analytical thoughts to choose in duality, experiencing between this and that for its likes and dislikes, creating a cause-and-effect relationship—consciously or otherwise.

The second illusion occurs because of emotionally identifying and attaching thoughts to your memory—I, me, and mine. Consciousness relates in duality to this physical self; subconsciously creating dependency, anxiety, and expectations. This phenomenon is imperative for your material becoming-ness to attach and accumulate. Both the mind and spirit get imprisoned to your desires and emotions, making you a slave of your subconscious beliefs. The mind ignores you are that ultimate potential, which is beyond all beyond, whether of knowledge or for any existence. You are that Creator, creation, and the basis of all forms of knowledge by the presence of that aware universal energy. It is knowledge that defines any existence, and the essence of that knowledge emerges only from awareness. In this circularity lies the ground of everything, which is nothing but awareness.

The third reason for illusions to arise is because of negativity and fear. Because of ego, the mind primarily survives on insecurity, leading to negativity and fear. Your thoughts subconsciously revolve around beliefs of how better you are or can become from the rest. Both negativity and fear are survival tactics for the mind for the sake of self-interest in self-preservation. While thinking negatively about others, you separate yourself from that inclusiveness, and the element of fear always connects to a future feeling, submerged in wants. To counter these two overpowering emotions—desire and fear—we have only one adhesive, which is love, but unfortunately this, too, has become conditioned with expectations, inciting jealousy and hurt. Negativity amplifies under fear; this includes anger, jealousy, greed, envy, hatred, anxiety, depression, etc. They create shades of doubt in your mind, and this happens only when love is absent. Love is that ultimate ingredient of oneness, the ultimate connection from which we attach to detach.

Therefore, *intense witnessing of your thinking self* is the real freedom from all bindings, attachments, conditioning, beliefs, and prejudices. It awakens that divine, the real you, the spirit lying dormant within. The mind awakens from its past conditioning and becomes aware of its actual self, wherein there is no duality. It makes you independent and free from your mind, and thinking provides alternatives, allowing you to choose between this and that, primarily to expand from your material wants.

Thoughts always arise from the past, deriving its data from the memory and the intellect, and after that it mulls over jumping from one aspect to another . . . projecting the same into the future. In contrast, awareness is always in the present, spontaneous, and immediate. Moreover, thoughts are mechanical and negative by nature. They are reflections of your mind's feelings that are heavily bent in your favour and for your kith and kin. They are unconscious by nature, emotional reactions, responding to external stimuli emerging out of your subconscious mind. The human brain is designed to operate mainly for its self-interest, always for pleasure and profits, never considering the needs of others. They occur *without* your conscious self being aware of them. For instance, if, in anger, you were aware and conscious, you would have known the cause of that anger and that itself would have enabled you to manage and handle that anger in the right manner.

The role of the spirit is to make your mind aware in order to check and guide the mind through its consciousness. In mental chatter, thoughts arise mechanically and answer subconsciously from the past, which is generally pessimistic and insecure, inviting fear. There are two ways to handle this situation. First, be alert and observant to witness every negative flow of thoughts. After that, consciously question the reason for its emergence and provide answers to put an end to that flow. Second, now, since you are aware and conscious of its pattern, compel and argue with your mind how to solve the issue so that it does not crop up again. In both the cases, awareness is that neutralizer, which brings forth answers to all that you subconsciously chatter in your mind.

Our emotions are biased in our favour, justifying and condemning others, especially when the mind is angry, jealous, desirous, greedy, etc. They arise from the past without your permission and behave subconsciously. Awareness, in this case, is absent; your body and mind may be active, but the *presence of you*—the soul (individuated expression of the spirit)—is asleep. If your mind is alert and attentive, the presence of the spirit within the soul is aroused. The mind becomes spontaneously aware, without analyzing your mind, it consciously knows and experiences and pro-acts sensitively instead of reacting sentimentally to that stimulus.

It is the same with love. Unconsciously, the mind is in love only with the body, conditioned and rigid with passion and lust; distorted in wants, possessive, remaining insecure. In awareness, love is innate, inborn, and intuitive . . . thoughtless on its flow. This sort of occurrence is in the moment of now, existential love, meaning, from one moment to the next, as it is, the way it is in that present moment. Psychological love arises from the abundance of ego—possessive and selfish. Spiritual love emerges from that ocean of oneness— total awareness, neither demanding, wanting nor expecting anything in return. It flows spontaneously. You *sensitively* and consciously become that love, totally involved, and not out of *sentimentality* . . . neither emotional nor selfish. You are merely giving without any expectations.

Love insists on freedom; it should not be tied or bound to the emotional, desirous mind. The mind separates every form of energy in duality with its opposite, hatred, lurking behind to overpower anytime. You, as the spirit, do not possess the other; you love for the sake of loving with no demands, conditions, rules, or terms. It is the mind, which is conditional and demanding. Absolute love is nothing but being consciously aware of your mind and its feelings. It is awake in the present, not thinking in selectivity, merely wishing to give in totality with no attachments or tags. It derives pleasure in giving as well as in receiving.

When the personal self, say, is eating, exercising, or engaging in any subconscious activity, you are not conscious. The spirit at this moment is dormant. Your mind is merely performing out of habit, subconsciously multitasking into this or that for likes and dislikes. It is only later when the mind is fully alert, attentive, and focused, meaning, it is still and silent on any act it experiences . . . how awareness (the spirit) turns the mind into a creative force of power, making it dynamic. Those daily routines, which your mind subconsciously enacts, tend to detach your spirit away and instead lean towards the ego-consciousness. Unpretentiously and unconsciously, your mind is thinking of multiple things while performing subconsciously.

Your mind is subconsciously familiar from past awareness to all that is around from its memory. The thinking self emanates from the memory and intellect, continuously chattering in subconscious thoughts. Meaning, in such moments, the presence of your individuated awareness is not aware of that presence. As a substitute, mindfulness is nothing but being meditatively (silently and effortlessly) aware from one moment to the next. It is from the above-mentioned that many neuroscientists claim that over 95 per cent of the time, the mind is functioning unconsciously, from its subconscious mind. Yes, they are correct! And it is for this very reason we have so much imbalance between the material and the spiritual. Materially, we have reached the sky; spiritually, we are doomed.

The mind, in its thoughts, endures from the past and handcuffs the future, relying on past events. Memory belongs to your past experiences. Consciousness, too, belongs to your past—meaning, the mind lives in the past. It is only the presence of your awareness, which is in the present, the now. For instance, truth and love are experiences of the now. However, the moment you think and put them into words, they go into the past, and an unconscious interpretation of your biased mind comes forth, losing its essence. Love and truth start to differ from one another, separating itself from that oneness of its manifestation. When you feel emotionally, biased words simply dilute the totality of oneness in the mind into its duality.

Please remember, awareness creates that spontaneous inner connection, via the soul, between you—the subject—with the object, the way you are and the way the issue is in the present . . . as one and not two. In such a case, spiritualism claims that the observer (the individual spirit) observing (through the mind) the observed (the object under observation) becomes one, unified in continuity.

Therefore, when you continuously witness your mind, you are in choiceless thoughts during any present moment, without any preconditions. Your presence is in total self-observation without depending on any psychic feelings or analytical thoughts. The former is the role of the spirit and the latter is thoughts to the mind. However, when you are thinking, there is an involvement of ego functioning from its past with earlier awareness. The spirit, in such cases, gets trapped in body-mind consciousness under the aura of self-gratification. It cannot be you but only the presence of body and mind acting unconsciously without the spirit. It is only that made-up version of you and not your true self that is identified with a body-mind in a name and gender, separated from that witness-er (Sakshi)—the soul containing the spirit.

Free your imprisoned spirit from that illusory thinking self with all its bindings and attachments of this and that. Only then will you come to know and clearly understand *who* you are. You are the presence of that pure, pristine, and present aware energy, which makes your mind aware of all that it perceives and conceives. It is the *means and the end* of your physical presence in this existence. Life without awareness is lifeless. Self or ego-consciousness merely contain memories of the past that instil fear. It reminds you of past karmas, making you doubtful and cautious for its future. It provides memories of previous awareness. You need to be aware and conscious in the now. Elevate, evolve, and effectuate your ego consciousness to a higher level. It is for this reason ancient sages declared the body-mind is nothing without the conscious principle until it *qualifies* to experience and realize the third dimension—the true self as the spirit.

When we say 'Thou Art That—Tat Tvam Asi', it means you are that material cause in unqualified pure consciousness as well as a part of that potential, efficient cause residing dormant as the formless, absolute individual spirit. Lord Krishna said that the body and mind are only the means. You first need to *understand* the whole concept of life to accomplish that end, which is of pure consciousness. As mentioned earlier, you do not need to become aware to be aware; it is your mind that needs to become aware and conscious. You are already that absolute awareness in the form of the spirit, and the mind is ignorant about that. It just does not know how to comprehend and coax the spirit. Your presence of awareness is required to move effortlessly on its own because the moment there is any effort, the order comes directly from the cognitive mind, not from the spirit.

You are that ultimate reality, the presence of awareness, which makes your mind aware and conscious. When you watch, observe, or witness through the mind at any existential moment, you are independent of any thoughts or emotions. The mind, at this moment, is unable to affect you. Feelings persist or sustain only later when the flow of thoughts—the secondary 'thinker'—identifies, attaches, and clings to what it desires. Watching creates a gap between you and the thinker, thinking in personal or biased thoughts. So, be alert and aware, allow the mind to operate while in the presence of you; the spirit clearly witnesses every activity silently and effortlessly.

There is tension when the mind is rigid on what it wants or in the grip of anxieties about future thoughts. Release that tension. Allow the mind complete freedom to move in what it wants to. Just observe . . . meaning, witness the wanting mind. However, this becomes possible only if you understand with clarity that you are not the mind but the spirit individuated as the soul or witnessing self. They are two sides of the same coin, one end you have the witnessing self and on the other the ego-self.

Awareness is that force, which radiates a field of conscious energy. Like the sun is that force from which the light energy illuminates the earth. Just keep witnessing inwards, and the authentic truth, reality, love, and sensitivity will lead your mind towards being free . . . away from those personal thoughts. They gradually transform into their absoluteness. Just keep observing in and out, always be alert and attentive. Expanding is the basic nature of energy while doing so; it also evolves and transforms the mind to rise higher from its material ego-consciousness, especially if you are seeking mental peace and tranquillity to counter agitations of the mind.

The sun, by itself, does not perform any action; it only radiates its field of energy. Similarly, awareness on its own is not aware of itself but makes the mind aware of its field of consciousness. Awareness is absolute, total, passive, limitless, timeless, spaceless, and independent, not requiring any support, whereas consciousness is dependent and dual by nature, requiring awareness for its support. It reveals itself as the Creator embedded in every creation.

You are that unchanging state of 'I-lessness' in the form of awareness and not that ever-changing body and mind, which your mind presumes to be. The brain and its thoughts belong to your individual soul, that Sakshi (witness-er), but they aren't *you*. You, as that spirit, retain your absoluteness in all respects and do not keep changing as the mind does from child to ego-consciousness. It is within the presence of your soul (witnessing consciousness) that changes take place and subside in the same. You remain as that sky and the ocean, where all changes occur like clouds or waves moving here and there, now and then. It requires consciousness to experience through the mind to engage your true presence. When the mind and body die, consciousness—like the shining light energy emanating from the sun—dissipates in the vast expanse of the universe, and what remains is only that eternal, infinite aware energy.

Your experiences may transcend from one beyond to another. You are the potentiality of that ultimate knowledge, which requires no further transcendence. Your mind and consciousness are supposed to explore and discover that uniqueness with the aid of the presence of your true self through which the mind experiences and realizes to go beyond. Therefore, within that mind and body, you reside as absolute awareness, the prime reason to be associated and attributed as 'Thou Art That'.

Chapter 11

HOW TO BECOME THE
MASTER OF YOUR LIFE

'If you wish to be free,
Know you are the self.
The witness of all these,
The heart of awareness.'

—Paramhansa Yogananda, Ashtavakra Gita

(1.3)

𝒥N ORDER TO UNDERSTAND LIFE, IT IS ESSENTIAL THAT WE
first grasp the concept of duality. Duality means two, and the
human mind correspondingly functions or determines only
after separating the absolute energy in its relative opposites of
two. For example, to know about heat, it is necessary for the
brain to compare it with cold. In this manner, we have God/
devil, good/bad, birth/death, positive/negative, happiness/
sadness, etc. They are like dual wings of a bird, which interact
with each other, creating a balance in every aspect of life. Only
after that can the mind come to any conclusion. This separation
gives the human mind the power of choice. However, though
the power to choose makes them superior to all other living
creatures, duality also makes them susceptible to all sorts of
conflicts while choosing this or that for selfish reasons.

Likewise, for everything the mind seeks, it separates the
oneness of every aspect into a subject-object relationship. The

brain needs to create this separation in every form of energy to understand the known from its unknown. Meaning, the *knower* (self/soul) as the subject *knowing* through the mind creates that separation from the *known*, the object in question. Thus, the job of the brain is to separate the absoluteness of every attribute of energy into its objective duality. The moment the mind transcends duality, it begins to understand its true nature of oneness—the absolute spirit embedded in the mind. It is that which remains constant and does not change like the mind does. This disposition creates the basic difference between the material mind and the spiritual self.

Non-dualism means one without a second—changeless and constant, the noumenal essence underlying all creations. The phenomenal world, on the other hand, is full of dualities. In the former, we have what has been considered as the highest attribute of energy, the eternal spirit of awareness, the infinite un-manifested energy remaining absolute and non-dual. Whereas, in the latter, we have interchangeable subset energies as the finite manifested as matter and consciousness that are limited within space, time, and causation. Both are real and exist as one, it is just that both matter and consciousness are superimposed on the spirit, which, in our case, is that broad substrate comprising the principle of awareness or that being-ness in life, which embraces and unfolds all that exists in the universe.

Both Osho and J. Krishnamurti have spoken a lot on this subject-object relationship, claiming that the observer is the observed. Meaning, so long as observing thoughts do not disturb the absolute into duality, the observer remains as one in unity and continuity with that object being observed in choiceless awareness. After all, the thinker is but a culmination of thoughts presenting itself as that remember-er in the memory of the cognitive mind. It is only the mind or what it contains—thoughts—that disturbs this unity, separating everything in two to relate, choose, experience, and infer for self-gratification and self-preservation.

Therefore, on the *intellectual* front what we have are thoughts from the memory separating the oneness of all that it perceives into dual living. However, from the point of view of the witness-er, observation is non-dual and pure, creating that *intelligence* or instinct, which is spontaneous and immediate. This sort of observation is in choiceless thoughts where both the subject and the object are one in their absoluteness without any evaluation to disturb their unity. Since this book stresses a lot upon the cruciality of 'observation', let us ponder further on the factor of oneness from the point of view of an observer (individual) observing (through the mind in duality) the observed (the object) related to the study of spiritualism.

Whenever there is a motive behind any seeking, a separation in duality emerges between the subject and the object. A certain level of self-interest arises. The mind analyzes from its memory and intellect on the object of desire, separating the oneness of any form of energy into two in order to relate one from another. It also requires time to decipher how to choose in self-interest for a particular motive created by its intellect through desires and emotions. In this case, what we have here is the presence of a thinker *reacting* to emotions generated by the mind on how to experience the situation, consciously or otherwise.

However, if we continually watch our mind simply witnessing our thoughts while multitasking and experiencing desires, nonjudgmental and choiceless thoughts emerge. The mind, instead of multitasking, becomes conscious and acts with single-pointed attention. Instead of reacting, the mind now begins to spontaneously pro-act. In such cases, the subject and the object remain one without any separation between them.

Therefore, by nature, a spiritual person will not wish to practise methods dictated by thoughts of desires in his or her mind, for they are mainly in separation for the sake of self-interest. Through his or her higher capacity of observation, he or she effortlessly silences the process of thinking. The observer effect demonstrates that simply observing any situation brings about changes to what is being observed. According the Weizmann Institute of Science, 'By the act of sheer watching, the observer affects the observed reality.' Similarly, when we continuously witness our thoughts that are randomly chattering about past and future, they become *still*. Relative thinking in duality stops on its own, without any choice or effort. The observer and the observed dissolve in their oneness with sheer *observation*. Hence, it is *observation* that embodies the presence of universal aware energy wherein there is an absence of any 'I'. It does not comprise thoughts in 'you and me', just waves of energy selflessly performing its role—making the mind aware, revealing all that exists is not two.

When the mind operates and experiences anything, there is a duality between the experiencer and on what one experiences. However, to be spiritual, there cannot be any duality; the spirit is one and only understands oneness. If you wish to awaken that spirit seated within, the observer (individual) observing (mind) the observed (object) needs to be one in their absoluteness. You will need to respect both with grace as one and not two, both being two sides of the same coin. For an observer, both God and devil is one, and so is heaven and hell. It is your mind creating that separation for its own convenience to determine and choose between what is moral and immoral.

All three—body, mind, and spirit—need to become one. In the ultimate reality, all that exists is one in the eternal now, as it is, existentially, for the duration that it exists . . . without you and me requiring to think and tell what it is. Meaning, for experiencing materiality, we need duality because for the spiritual, there exists only oneness. Thus, the phenomenal attributes of all objective/material existences occur within space and time due to causation. These are *illusory* appearances happening in your consciousness, which the subjective presence, the noumenon, the spirit of total awareness simply observes through the mind of any living creature in order to experience what we call life.

Essentially, just the subject of total awareness exists. The universe unfolds solely because we, as body and brain, can observe to make the mind aware of all that exists. The ultimate reality is that unchanging substratum without constraints of any space or time, within which all transient existences are superimposed to appear and disappear for the duration they exist. These transitory manifestations in the forms of solids, liquids, and gases are interchangeable, but they remain indivisible within the infinite substrata of the absolute pure energy. Thus, intellectually, there is a constant change in all that exists; to exist itself is a transient change from its absolute eternal reality to experience its attributes and return into the same. I refer to this temporary phenomenon as mid-reality, which is also real but, temporarily, in a different aspect.

Therefore, spiritually, you are not the seer (observer) or the seeing (mind), nor are you the seen (object). You, as the spirit, are merely that presence of total aware energy, and the observer is that individualized soul *witnessing* through the operating system of the brain everything that the body and mind wish to experience or see—without thinking, analyzing, condemning, judging, accepting, or rejecting. You, in an I-less state of being-ness, are that spirit spontaneously involved in what is being observed, as one. Like when you are intensely watching a flower or a sunset on the sea, your mind instinctively is in awe, conjoined to what is being observed, with zero thinking. *Reduce* the prowess of your analytical thinking to compare and choose this or that, become spiritual. Move from the intellectual to the instinctual. Let this be your mantra.

The mind is an operating system working on electromagnetic-chemical fields of energy. It requires awareness to move its other forms of energies like emotions and desires. Aware energy keeps manifesting in the mind whenever the mind observes. Initially, there is no choosing, conflict, or separation; it is simply aware. Immediately after that, it extends; the mind becomes conscious and attaches to dual thinking. It takes time for the conscious or the subconscious areas to react upon the same. The flow of thoughts is a process in unity of one thought meeting another, or one desire attracting another to react upon the same emotionally. Physically, the brain exists; the mind does not as it is merely a multiprocessor software system.

However, when you watch and witness your mind and its thoughts, it becomes shy, still, and aware of being watched. Thoughts of the past and future begin to fade, replacing them with thoughtless awareness. You enter into the present mode just for that short moment. Nobody can control the mind; it continues to unconsciously operate on its own from past to future thoughts unless the spirit interferes, watching over the same. In such a situation, the mind gets disturbed and distracted and becomes conscious. This changes its mechanical motion of activity. While simply observing, you can silently watch the movements of your thoughts—they become still, and you are in direct contact with the concerned object. The duality between the observer and the observed . . . the subject and the object diminishes. There is no individual effect or any separation or conflict; you spontaneously pro-act on any situation without the need for any separation. *Constantly witnessing your mind is considered to be spiritual, the rest are all material conceptualizations devised by the mind.*

Beyond the mind, there is nothing, just a vast sea of emptiness. You may only divert, distract, and divulge the brain but only through another part of the mind. Witnessing the mind makes it more dynamic, for, in that present moment, the mind becomes aware and *superconscious*. It merely changes the mode of operation, from working mechanically to mindfully. When you watch and witness, there is spiritual progress. You look inwards into your thoughts, the whole perception changes, random thoughts dissipate. You become alert, attentive, and aware. A transformation takes place. Natural or existential thoughts originate from your sensory perception about the outer world. Choiceless thoughts prevailing at any present moment are simply the presence of your actual self as the soul acting merely as the observer.

Those who spend time silently, in the company of their true self, minimize thoughts that helps them in many ways. Not only do they assess past and future thoughts, but also become an impartial and impersonal witness of the outer world. They remain dispassionate in what they experience, remaining non-attached and nonjudgmental, being mindfully present in their true self. Highly successful people are ordained with such traits, whereas others do so intermittently. However, it is welcome to all, who lucidly understand the true self spiritually. After knowing the power of witnessing, they effortlessly begin to improve and mature from the inside out. Effortless witnessing is a simple assertion of intuitive experiencing—simple and clear. Since this does not provide any *masala* to spiritual masters, marketers, or artistes, the Ashtavakra Gita has never been strongly advocated or preached as compared to the well-known Bhagavad Gita or Ramayana.

An immoral person, in my opinion, in some ways is better than those who claim to be honest, religious, or spiritual. At least, he or she is aware and knows what he or she is and would have better chances if and when he or she chooses and intends to evolve and transform. However, there are many, as we all know, who live in ignorance, with illusions of being moral, ethical, religious, or presuming to be spiritual. Firstly, they are not aware of their true self and secondly, just by claiming so to others, one does not become moral.

Knowing, preaching, or following any religious text narrating Sanskrit words do not make you spiritual. Also, for that matter, nor doing any motivational mental practices can make you one. So long as you promote your name and identity to the outer world, whether a guru or a disciple, you remain in the sphere of that central processing unit called the ego-mind. Your mind sustains and survives in illusions with consent, compulsions, and conflicts of what you are not, which, of course, includes myself while writing this book.

When you are with the world, thinking is prime. However, inner or self-observation should always be continuous at all times while one is thinking and experiencing for the sake of that self-awakening. You can awaken the presence of your being-ness just by remaining alert and observant—watching and witnessing those inner thoughts passing by. The brain does not permit any checks, brakes, or control of its random and reckless multitasking behaviour. I repeat, you need to observe, watch, and witness the subconscious thoughts continuously in order to make your mind *aware* of what it is about to invoke and implement. This shall make the mind *conscious* of its conduct, thereby enriching your thoughts.

The cognitive mind deals only with the past and future limiting the mind, whereas the spirit is for the present moment. It functions, unfortunately, like a pendulum swinging from one end to another, without stopping in the centre, which represents that present moment. What your mind really needs to learn and practise is the effortless and straightforward method of mindfulness—being in meditative awareness from one moment to the next, watching and witnessing persistently.

The flow of the mind is the consequence of time. The thinker survives mainly in the past taking continuous support from its memory. From the memory section of the brain, you remember your name, identity, address, and everything that the mind thinks to project into its future. Consciousness resides in the mind as that *remember-er* in the form of self-consciousness. In such a manner, spontaneous or immediate thoughts in the form of intelligence, instinct, or intuition emerge in the present moment, whereas past to future thoughts arise from the intellect with data supplied by the memory. All three conjoin to enable the mind to expand, evolve, and transcend from the unknown into the known, what we commonly refer to as simple common sense.

The knowing arises out of that *unknowable* (aware energy), the intensity of which determines an individual's level of unique intelligence at any given moment. Hence, the presence of that awareness is the subject or the context of *who you are*, and consciousness is the object or the content of *what you are*, through your memory. An awakened awareness (Chaitanya) is the one that is beyond such illusions and spiritually knows the true nature of its own reality. This we refer to as self-knowledge.

Your mental attitude originates from your habits. Habits are developed from past actions, gradually making up the quantum of what you are in ego-consciousness. Patterns consequently get programmed as beliefs within your mind. They emerge and dictate your material existence, becoming your nature to do so. Habit is an unconscious state of mind victimizing you from past actions to create a wheel of constant repetition. Karma, on the other hand, is a culmination of activities originating from previous genes combined with the beliefs of now along with your desirous actions and attitude towards the future. It reveals: As you sow, so shall you reap. Therefore, always be alert and watchful to witness your karmas, and not to make them go astray under continuous self-observation.

You as a flow of *aware* energy embedded in the mind is that subject, which is aware of its object—the body and mind. All you need to do is to *awaken* the presence of this aware energy (spirit) in order to make the mind aware and conscious of all it thinks, knows, and experiences. However, due to ignorance of this self-knowledge, the thinking self starts to *become* something known as the self-consciousness. The unchanging 'I', that impersonal, I-less state of being-ness (no-self) dilutes to become 'me', and the mind further begins to perceive from its 'mine' (my thoughts) and falsely—through self-consciousness—considers that to be 'myself'.

Even in such cases, the true self (observer-individual soul) remains aloof from the three well-known states of consciousness—dreaming (unfulfilled wants), deep sleep (unconscious state), and awake (for the external world). However, it is the fourth state, *turiya* (pure consciousness), the true self as the Sakshi (observer), permeates the other three states through sheer witnessing and watching the entire drama of life played by the other three states for its illusory— me and mine. Therefore, as mentioned earlier, the presence of this aware cosmic energy residing within the soul is that being- ness of who you are, which merely watches and witnesses. The individual intensity of aware energy is later responsible for creating that uniqueness or individuality of any human being for its becoming-ness from its self-consciousness.

Consequently, self-consciousness is that quantum of past conditioning from habits of any human mind that makes you *what* you are. And it is the awareness of now that makes your mind aware of *who* you are—a state of being-ness. Hence, try not to be critical or condemn anything. Do not attach to any emotion or identify what is transient. It is that true self, the witnessing self, which reveals all that is there to see in this universe. Because from the universal point of view, what exists is only that nothingness in silence. The universe, on its own, does not exist. It is that individual state of being-ness, the essence of all perception, the witnessing self, which unfolds and permits the physical senses to observe and apprehend all that it perceives and conceives of the universe.

I repeat, the I-less state representing total awareness entrapped in any individual soul is the only true existence, which is responsible for unravelling all that is present in the universe. Meaning, the soul being the observer is that foremost representative, which holds the individual intensity of aware energy in any body and mind.

Total awareness is the highest unchanging attribute of energy compared to numerous diverse forms of subset energies of the universe. The rest being transient are what we conceptualize with names like nuclear, thermal, hydro, electrical, etc., providing interchangeable forms of gases, liquids, and solids. They superimpose sub-atomically in the forms of particles and waves, eventually to return to nothing but dark energy.

Every knowledge for the mind depends upon its subject-object relationship. Supreme knowledge, in our case, is that total awareness, the sole subject, which transcends all other attributes of matter and consciousness. It is that ultimate knowledge, and when all knowledge comes to an end, what remains is simply nothing but truth. There is no further going or attaining anything beyond that ultimate truth.

Therefore, your material 'I' remains in self-consciousness until you die and dissipate after the death of the body and mind into that expanse of the infinite aware energy as one. All transitory attributes of energy-matter and consciousness eventually wither into that absolute oneness of nothing (shunya). There cannot be any universal consciousness because the absolute energy is neither aware nor conscious of itself. It is passive and dormant on its own; however, it has the ability to make the mind aware and conscious. It is capable of making every microscopic living cell of organisms, including the macroscopic mind, aware and conscious.

The presence of this supreme divine energy awakens to its highest level only in the human brain, empowering the human mind not only to be aware of the outside but also to be aware of its inner thoughts and consciousness. For this reason, we are potentially accredited as Aham Brahmasmi, Shivohum, Tat Tvam Asi, or Thou Art That. This individual part of the potential supreme energy, if awakened, permits the human mind to explore and discover the infinite possibilities of the universe and the meaning behind God as well.

When non-dual aware energy spontaneously manifests in the mind, further continuing into thoughts, the aware mind, in turn, separates the non-dual into its duality to choose, infer, and experience for its self-interest in self-consciousness. Aware energy is absolute and universal, whereas self-consciousness is dual, containing past awareness. I repeat, until the mind exists, consciousness exists, too. Awareness is that *drive* (motion of energy) and consciousness is that *driver* driving through mind with awareness, consciously or subconsciously. The drive always remains, but the driver vanishes after the death of body and mind.

However, it is claimed by many that when consciousness becomes pure, it realizes to be at par with total awareness (Parabrahman), the absolute supreme self, which in my opinion, is actually not possible. The Antaratma in such self-realization is supposed to have accomplished the status of the Paramatma. Consciousness, in such purity, becomes more of a guiding light, an inspiration, which in my opinion, is physically not realizable by the mortal living self. In such a case, the body, mind, and soul need to become one in a non-dual state of absoluteness, i.e., Parabrahman. It is that final state of self-realization wherein the individual soul realizes absolute energy in totality as one with the supreme prior to death. This is more of a visionary concept of oneness in absoluteness . . . experientially not realizable.

Coming back to our mortal self, if you do not engage in your desirous thoughts identifying and attaching, submerged in subconscious activities, you become free from externalities. When the mind is observing independently, thoughts resign, and the spirit awakens. The past, present, and future become one in existential moments. *From the limited mind, you enter into a state of limitlessness.* You only watch and witness, allowing the mind to play its game of illusions. Your job is to watch that mind wishing to become something. The more you watch, the more you remain free and independent of all its anxieties about the future and sufferings of its past.

Allow the mind to become *something* while it is kicking and alive. It is the function of the brain to expand, evolve, and effectuate into *becoming* something. Celebrate because you are only a witness to all that is happening; try not to attach to that psychophysical self. Keep this in mind, so long as the mind is dependent on the external world, it will not permit a selfless attitude, nor will it allow it to detach from its style of dual living. It thrives and survives only by choosing and clinging to this or that in selfishness.

The cognitive mind is clearly not designed for selflessness; it entraps the conscious and subconscious levels. This imbalance of being overly selfish and overwhelmed with a personal ego makes it imperative for us to know and lucidly understand the superconscious level. This is why you notice selfishness and self-centredness prevailing all around. Try and cultivate some habits of humility in being selfless as much as you can. But if you think you have fully succeeded, as many masters surmise, please witness your inner-self truthfully. Only the superconscious section of the mind has this ability to watch and witness, uninvolved and unaffected by the brain, and this happens only if you are alert and attentive in total silence, which itself is extremely difficult. If it were that easy, there would not be so much mess or misery all around.

A person remains a victim of his or her past and a *slave* to his or her future but becomes a *master* only if he or she is in the present. This can be determined by how observant you are of your mind, which, in turn, makes you what you are. However, the fundamental problem of life is that we keep blaming and judging others, shirking from our responsibilities. Life is made up of choices, and we are required to consciously choose one out of every duality responsibly. Your ability to respond to those choices determine whether they shall bring forth inclusiveness or divisiveness. It is entirely dependent on how mindful (immediate awareness) you are of what you feel, think, say, and act, and whether your mind is observant and aware of all those above-mentioned factors?

Watch and witness. The past will disappear, the present will appear; allow your mind to be aware and conscious. A person of awareness continuously observes and pro-acts in spontaneity. A person who is not aware becomes unconscious, broods, and reacts in a biased manner after thinking emotionally to satiate what he or she desires. Your self-consciousness accordingly reflects what you are, either in selfishness with incoherence or responsibly in cohesion. It reveals and reflects *what* you are at that moment, the way a mirror does. The mind is like a photo plate that keeps memorising pictures of the past, reflecting your cumulative personality through your self-consciousness either in divinity or in devilishness.

Life is certain; it is your mind that remains uncertain, continuously changing due to its constant desires and uncontrollable emotions. Be responsible; do not blame others. Surrender your mind and accept the present moment as it is, without any justification. It is your existentialism that decides, not your mind. Thinking is essential for your material expansion. Responsibility demands both material as well as spiritual growth in cohesiveness. This makes you holistically evolve and transform like a tightrope walker balancing both ends with a pole.

Thinking can make you a great material person. Being a silent watcher inside out will make you a master of your life. Accommodate both in their balanced perspective. Dreams are your unfulfilled desires; awareness is your spiritual insight amid material unfulfillment. You must live as if there is no past or future. The past was once the present, and the future will become the present. If the present, meaning now, is complete and durable, the other two converge as one. The material manifestation in such a manner evolves with spiritual progress in a holistic responsibility to care for all as one in totality. When the mind mainly thinks of the past and future, which it usually does, it misses the present, which is so crucial. For a spiritualist, mind is a hindrance, continually chattering about the past, always anxious about its future, completely missing the now. This unconscious process imbalances the mind. We need to conjoin all three—body, mind, and soul—for a fulfilled, balanced life.

Chapter 12

THE TWO MINDS

*'When I have realized the Witness, the Supreme
Self, the Lord,
And when all longing for release and bondage
has gone,
There is no anxiety for emancipation.'*
—Baij Nath, The Ashtavakra Gita

IT IS DIFFICULT TO SIN WHEN YOUR MIND IS AWARE AND conscious of what you are about to do, unless the desire is too strong. In fact, there is no such thing as right or wrong or good and bad as both are two sides of the same coin. It is in the absence of one the other exists, like in the absence of light, darkness prevails. They are a matter of individual opinion based on beliefs depending, again, upon particular situations and personal judgements. Morality depends upon what you are conscious about—material or spiritual. In the case of the spiritual, all is one so long as your soul is constantly witnessing what your mind is doing.

Everything in the universe is one solitary absolute energy, or what the ancient sages referred to as Brahman flowing as waves of energy in unity and continuity as one. Energy can neither be created nor destroyed; it cannot be even divided. It exists merely as it is in its absoluteness, remaining constant, one without a second. However, within itself, it interchanges from one form into another—from gases, liquids, to solids.

The world is an exemplification of this unified indivisible absolute energy, symbolizing myriad forms of living and non-living transient subset energies, which are superimposed on that one without a second. Human beings are one such living example with the highest developed brain—possessing the capacity of speech; abstract reasoning out of memory, intellect, and intelligence; and the awareness of being conscious not only of the outside world but also the inner composition of its own body and mind.

The inquiry into the nature of this ultimate reality with respect to the manifestation of this absolute energy, Brahman, in multitude forms of creation has been the centre of contemplations in the study of Vedanta, asserting many speculative positions of Vedantic thoughts going back over thousands of years. In short, though the absolute is devoid of all diversities, yet all diversities emanate from the same. Like the fluid in the egg of a peacock is colourless, but all the colours of the peacock emanate from this very liquid.

The contention here is both the *nirguna* (absolute—non-dual) and the *saguna* (with personal attributes of duality) are intertwined and are mere projections of the one behaving as two. Implying that the supreme attribute of the nirguna in its dormant form is that of Parabrahman (total awareness), and the highest attribute of saguna in its active form is the potentiality of becoming Paramatma (pure consciousness). Both suggest the manifestation of bliss from the supreme energy in a state of formlessness and represent God in the latter form as well.

As energy beings, the absolute divine form manifests and activates in the mind in the form of awareness, which has the ability to unfold all that the mind sees, hears, and describes. We as humans have this divine potentiality of making our mind aware and conscious to advance, expand, and evolve in any direction that the mechanical mind subconsciously perceives and conceives. Meaning, we should keep in mind that unless a living entity is aware, there is neither any perception nor existence.

This aware energy, when it penetrates the human mind, is initially absolute and spontaneous, but after continuing into analytical thoughts, the mind separates this non-dual energy into its duality in opposites to choose, experience, infer, and realize either consciously or subconsciously with unconscious thoughts. Meaning, if the mind is attentive after becoming aware, it is conscious, otherwise, it majorly functions in an unconscious manner from its subconscious section. Therefore, depending on the state of mind's attentiveness at any given space and time, the direction of its focus, as given by neuroscientists today, is over 95 per cent in the subconscious state. This, below the conscious level, is that of the thinking self, which we refer to as the ego or self-conscious state of mind. As a result, the intensity of this conscious factor in any individual mind from its suffix of -ness is that determinant factor of how thoughts visualize and experience—self-destructive or self-constructive. Meaning, depending on the attitude of a human mind (positive or negative), psychic energy vibrates and moves in higher or lower frequency accordingly, awakening the presence of any individual's awareness.

However, when the mind is unconscious, it functions mechanically in an auto mode from its subconscious section that derives data directly from the memory and the intellect. Unconsciously, not being attentive, the mind keeps imitating what it has learnt from the past. It may think of the future, but the continuity comes from the memory containing data of the past. Most of us emulate subconsciously, following what we have attained in the past, projecting the same into the future. The attitude of the mind in such cases *selfishly* revolves around how and in what direction the mind has developed its individual personality depending entirely upon what one believes, irrespective of its rationality. For this reason, we have far more negative aspects rather than positive ones, selfishly flowing, accumulating, and attaching to its material identity, *a thinking self* with a name provided by others and borrowed knowledge from its memory and intellect. Such is the law of nature, which unfortunately limits the limitless mind, functioning overly from its past, going directly into the future.

In self-obsession, we forget the millennium-old saying: 'Tat Tvam Asi—Thou Art That.' The universe exists because we say so. Similarly, the presence of God prevails because we have conceptualized him as the divine. Meaning, we are none other than that potential divine, which we exhibit and express, not with personal names or any gradings but in our acts of divinity. We have that supreme abstract energy imbibed in our soul, which we refer to as awareness. All depends upon how one utilizes this sovereign energy to expand, evolve, and transform to those heights of consciousness, say, of Buddha, Jesus, or in the devilish nature of demons.

Please remember, all thoughts and beliefs, for that matter, relate to the past, from where we turn our habits in attitudes, which by nature, are mostly unconscious. They are nothing but a mechanical way of reacting in an autopilot mode out of our memory and intellect, containing past data. I restate, we routinely, in a subconscious manner, think and act unconsciously that gradually turns into habits forming our attitude. Consequently, we become victims of our mental impressions, impact, or imprint called *samskaras*, meaning, karmas or actions emerging from our habits. It gives us that feeling of a doer, a culmination of unconscious thoughts functioning from its recollection of the past, seeking for something in the future.

Karma is relevant for the material world experiencing actions from cause and effect. It is intentional action emerging out of thoughts, and we are responsible for the same as it creates our future or destiny. It generates results according to our actions and is generally unconscious because we are normally semi-aware of most of our thoughts and actions.

Meaning, *it is our mind that is karmic.* The spirit, on the other hand, is that presence of awareness, which merely watches and witnesses, flowing along with the intensity of any material or spiritual awareness of an individual mind. From our karmas, habits are formed, developing later as our character, which is more of a false persona to show the illusory world how and what we are.

It is not the real us but that thinking self, playing imaginary games. If we wish to know and understand the true self, then the karmic theory is not relevant. It is meant for the outer or material life, the individual physical objective life going through an experiential stage in duality bound by self- or ego-consciousness, which, as mentioned earlier, is a stage of mid-reality. It is meant for those who are not aware of their absolute reality—the formless impersonal nature of our soul or that impartial witnessing self, which is that true self. All else is an illusion. The energy that moves through the cycle of birth and death in the form of body and mind is apparent (seems to be real, but is not), and as claimed both by spiritualists and scientists, is more of an optical illusion.

The actual *you* are that presence of awareness, a state of *I-less-ness*, merely a flow of aware energy, which we refer to as life, embodied in body-mind and soul, responsible for making all three awake and alive to experience the dualities of life, of which science as of today is ignorant. It is for this very reason, the subject of spiritualism insists upon the essentiality of acquiring the correct self-knowledge; in fact, quantum physics is making all attempts to come closer to it.

The thinking or the material self keeps developing habits throughout life—expanding, evolving, and effectuating as it advances and progresses. Relatively and reasonably concerned more for the outer, where conscience (sense of right and wrong) or morality plays a significant role to create a sort of balance between the good and bad habits. They are further reinforced by ethics, which are connected to moral principles laid down by those who govern and judge. Meaning, morality is more or less laid down by religion, and ethics is what the authorities enforce.

However, if and when, we are inwardly aware and conscious, not from the thinking mind (material) but from that witnessing mind (spiritual), there is an effortless awakening from what our individual consciousness does not agree to. Only then our mind is on a spiritual path towards that oneness of who and what we are, where there is no duality of this or that to segregate what our mind thinks to choose in selfishness.

As mentioned earlier, observing is what makes the mind aware, after that, it becomes conscious of perceiving and conceiving in any individual life. Awareness brings out that totality between the past, present, and future as one. It is that insight, which occurs spontaneously from moment to moment, awakening you from darkness to light. Hence, the sum of what you perceive consciously (inwards) as well as subconsciously (outwards) makes you *what you are* as a unique person in this world. It creates your individuality or that uniqueness, while you are physically active and alive.

Alertness and awareness, both, are synonymous to watchfulness. When the mind is alert to every thought, action, and deed, you think less, observe more, and enter into the present. You become spontaneous and proactive in choiceless thoughts. You become sensitive to every stimulus and respond naturally, meaning, existentially without reacting in any analytical thoughts. Watching is that supreme phenomenon, which brings in that clarity your mind requires.

In Physics, the mere observation of any phenomenon inevitably qualifies for that phenomenon, explained by the observer effect. Spiritually, it means the objective world around us materializes only after we are aware. It may be there, irrespective of our presence, but it only comes into light or existence after we become aware. Observation is that qualifying factor, for every seeing or experiencing, allowing the mind to become aware of all knowledge, which again is the basis for all existence. Hence, for both knowledge and existence, the prerequisite is awareness.

As you keep watching, the mind becomes, first, aware and, after that, conscious, which reduces unnecessary chattering. The spirit awakens, and the conscious mind starts to behave, say, if you know your body to be obese, keep watching your body—do not feel, think, or criticize. The mind shall become conscious, again and again, the thinking mind will, on its own, demand to eat less. Therefore, if you merely watch your action, in this case, while you eat without condemning or justifying, the witnessing mind will effortlessly make the thinking mind aware and conscious towards that fact.

Your becoming conscious is what makes you stronger with an inner inspiration. It is that clarity, which ushers in the truth, and that understanding, which comes from awareness. It removes all distortions of perceptions, bringing the thinker and his or her bundle of thoughts further towards the witnessing mind. *The essence of watching and witnessing are the only spiritual prerequisites you need to evolve from one moment to the next, where the observing mind is continuously alert on the thinking mind.*

Be always alert and attentive. You spontaneously pro-act to every moment from the intensity of your individual awareness and not from past recollections, habits, or memory. The outer energy responds to those frequencies of inner vibrations. The cosmic energy always responds with matching frequency to those of the inner self. Meaning, a *coherent* attitude with constructive *intention* will have positive results. To be spiritual indicates a *holistic* view of life, which shows effortless action from the mind, where you are *sensitive* and *responsive* to all as one, and continuously observant not to entertain any personal thoughts, which are harmful or destructive by nature.

You are not to resent, repent, or regret if experiences, mistakes, or actions are not in your favour. They are required more for the material world for making you expand in external fields. To excel in any objective field is an emotional desire for this or that, which are impulses coming from the selfish mind. Fresh awareness, say, instant knowing emerging from moment to moment, involves an alert mind that evolves the totality of any subject in choiceless thoughts. In such instances, your thoughts and actions are not biased for any analytical outcome.

On the contrary, if you listen and gossip about what the society projects and demands, your conscience will make you believe and follow what others want you to do. When truth recedes into belief, reality gets distorted, and we unnecessarily cling to what we believe. It is an unconscious state of mind, which deceives us from its actuality, gradually turning into faith. However, our true nature, that potential divine residing within, the spirit inside that *witnessing mind*, merely wants our thinking mind to be alert, attentive, and aware. Both need to be in coherence for a holistic life. So, watch and witness and allow the spiritual mind to spontaneously lead your material mind in order to celebrate this journey of life.

Religion is nothing but a myth. It is not a reality. It is borrowed, exhausted knowledge, or fables from the past, laying commandments for today. If you really wish to be religious, become selfless in religiosity, practising oneness in divinity. The divine being-ness is seated in the midst of awareness, which connects you to that whole in totality, with no ifs and buts—*Know Thyself*. You are that potential divine, a flow of pure aware energy, which we refer to as the spirit. The moment you know and understand your true self, your presence will reveal from that something towards that nothingness; you surrender your mind/ego and flow in divinity.

Your thinking mind is nothing but a bundle of fleeting thoughts. The thinking self survives and sustains primarily on blind beliefs, but this is not the case with the spiritual self, which only watches and witnesses. The thinking mind accumulates and borrows past data; the spiritual mind brings forth that creative and sublime energy. A mind is only an operating system of the physical brain acquiring information from its

RAM or memory, churning through its central processing unit (intellect) that programmed software downloaded from past inputs based on beliefs, desires, insecurity, negativity, and selfishness—all combined into fear and insecurity, wanting something in the future.

The emotional and desirous data is stored in that hard disk called the brain, within which flows a complex network of neurons through neural pathways, consisting of electromagnetic currents arising from chemical activity to process past data and put them into proper functioning. It has nothing of its own since the mind, on its own, does not physically exist. It is ignorant about the presence of its being-ness, the source of all-knowingness, which is the intensity of its individual aware energy signified from its suffix of -ness. Hence, in spite of being composed of such a profound set of cognitive faculties, the mind is ineffective and worthless, remaining mechanical unless the aware conscious principle—the being-ness—sets in. It makes the mind aware and conscious to know all that it knows from the planets to waves of eternal, infinite energy comprising the universe.

More than knowing, you will need to understand every aspect of life, from which your basic common sense emerges. Thoughts will continue to chatter and stay afloat only if you identify and attach to them. The spirit is not aware of itself. It requires an individual mind to awaken the spirit to make the mind, in turn, become aware and conscious. The role of the soul is merely to watch, observe, and witness your thoughts on the monitor of your brain.

When the mind observes any situation, it is that pure awareness (spirit) in its spontaneity; thoughtless thoughts plainly observing any situation. At this present moment of the eternal now, free from any space or time, you are independent from those anxious, desirous, emotional, and analytical thoughts. A unification occurs between the cognitive (thinking) and the soul (witnessing) mind. The mind, in turn, becomes aware of the outer and the inner with zero evaluation.

There is no desire or any dual-factor left to relate to. You, as the witnessing self, are now one with the thinking self. You are at peace within yourself without any demand. This state of mind is known as being spiritual . . . being your true self in the now.

Desires and emotions trigger more and more cravings. While this may be productive for the material self, it is detrimental to the synthesis of your inner with outer perceptions. Therefore, keep self-remembering (who you are) because you need to extend and expand those flashes of spontaneous creative awareness, occurring in the mind, into a constant flow. You should be able to awaken yourself to such an expanse that you become aware of your daydreaming and all those ridiculous acts of your mind resulting from its incessant desires. You need to become a watcher while breathing, eating, walking, and in every aspect of life. Your self-remembering and self-watching self-awakens that true self turning into a *self-reality*.

You will radiate a certain aura around yourself. Wherever you walk, people will notice you and will be touched inwardly by your presence. You will not be a thinker but a knower without thinking. You will know everything in totality, through your past, present, and future enacting in whole as one, where least resistance is required. This state of mind refers to being in choiceless thoughts, where you are choicelessly acting with spontaneous awareness proactively, rather than being fussy and reactive from emotional feelings full of desires.

Witnessing is that *quality* of mind, the context, which brings about creative intelligence in life. Thinking, on the other hand, is that *quantity* or the content of past information, the quantum of which brings about intellectuality in life. The witness (spirit) being passive only watches at any given moment and does not participate in any manner and remaining in its wholesomeness due to this reason. It does not have to think or act to separate the oneness of every energy in order to relate, define, and discern in relativity from its duality. The unity of energy in its totality remains permanent and real; separation done by the mind for its dual living is transient, hence, illusory. The fundamental characteristic of energy remains constant at all times in its absoluteness; the separation enacted by the mind is simply from the brain trying to appease itself to experience everything in its parts, rather than its whole.

The wholesomeness of any subject is of no concern to the cognitive mind. The job of the thinking mind is to separate the oneness of any subject; otherwise, the brain can't choose, evaluate, analyze, infer, experience, and realize one out of the two. It flows mechanically from the subconscious section; hence, it is beyond control. However, in the case of being spiritual, both the subject-object relationship remains intact in their wholesomeness while watching and, after that, pro-act spontaneously to go into action in choiceless thoughts. Therefore, a human mind is uncontrollable and infinite; however, it requires the divine residing within to awaken in order to supersede intellectuality in the form of a scholar and instead become a creative, intelligent being who is a leader amongst many and not a follower.

Thus, in order to experience life in totality, you need to experience both the material and the spiritual, the thinker as well as the observer. Both are essential parts of the same absolute spontaneity for the spiritual and relative thinking for cognition—so long as your third eye is continuously open. Do not negate any; accept both with grace and respect. Be continually aware and balanced to play the drama of life with poise and ease, like a tightrope walker witnessing and experiencing. Forget about becoming the divine, killing that ego, or suppressing any desire. Be humane to experience that humanness, for that is the true essence of life, which seems to be deteriorating day by day.

Chapter 13

CULTIVATING SPIRITUAL GROWTH

'You are Self—the Solitary Witness. You are
perfect, all-pervading, One. You are free,
desireless, forever still. The universe is but a
seeming in You.'

—Bart Marshall, Ashtavakra Gita (1.12)

*L*IFE IS A MOVEMENT OF ENERGY IN MATTER AND consciousness where both express their respective attributes. It determines your mind's vision and its attitude towards the meaning and purpose behind life. On its own, life has no meaning; it is your individuality while living that creates a meaning for you to become something. Spiritual life, on the other hand, is to know its actual source or that true self of infinite intelligence. It has no connection to any human god, religion, sect, cult, tradition, scriptures, books, or path. It is that pathless path of knowing yourself while making your mind compliant with the spirit. It necessitates comprehension, clarity, and clairvoyance in your material existence. In order to grow spiritually, what you require is to open your third eye (sixth sense), and the approach to do that is always be alert to watch and witness, with choiceless thoughts, both the aspects of life—the oneness of totality in a holistic manner and the awareness of the separation in duality to engage in a material life.

If you are alert, attentive, and aware, the mind consciously takes over thoughts that choose and experience either towards divinity or in the direction of the devil. Your awareness to understand and determine arises only after you observe both— the divine and the devil (dual living)—in order to cultivate a meaning and purpose of life. If it was only for that oneness, there would be no meaning for experiencing anything of life in duality. You are already that sky and the universe, then why would you need to observe and experience a drama called life where you need to relate every aspect with its opposite?

When you solely and spontaneously observe an object, it is in totality, on the other hand, what you experience the same in duality, it is in relativity. Since the observer is prior to all that you perceive, it signifies you are fundamentally a spiritual being and further validates that it is that spiritual aware energy, which wishes to experience and enjoy what life in duality is all about.

There is no method or path that your mind can undertake to be spiritual. You, as a physical thinking self with a name and gender, are the beginning and the end of your identity. The spirit does not require any direction, for it is eternally realized as the transcendent, which is encapsulated in the superconscious section of the mind as the witnessing self, which we refer to as the soul. It is the job of the mind to recognize and awaken that spirit lying dormant within the soul. The mind is phenomenal; the spirit is noumenal.

The mind has certain limitations because it subconsciously processes in selfishness from its past knowledge projecting that for its outcome in the future. All you need is to balance the mind with clarity and clairvoyance, activate the third eye— the observer or the awakened soul—to continuously witness in the present moment, celebrate the dualities of life to become something meaningful in this transient world. You have that potential ability of the divine but there is no need to try and become one. If you are ordained to become like Jesus or Buddha, no power on earth can stop you from becoming saintly or godly.

Spiritual growth is a pathless path; however, you definitely require a *path or a direction* to tame and discipline the material mind. To be spiritual, all you need is for your mind to be alert, observant, watch, and witness in order to effortlessly *awaken* the spirit to know how the brain is behaving itself. Whether it is Jnana, Karma, Raja, or Bhakti yoga, all are motivational efforts, methods, and techniques for that desirous mind to transcend towards higher consciousness in your material life. Your self-knowledge, self-awakening, and self-consciousness reflects how spiritual your mind has become towards that truth and unchanging reality, which the divine spirit is all about.

Therefore, you in that I-less state of being-ness are nothing but the spirit contained within an individual soul going through a human experience, empowered with the potentiality and the ability to be ascribed as 'Thou Art That'. Thou, here, refers to that divine experience beyond the comprehension of the mind, when one experiences that oneness with the one and only 'Paramatma' or 'Parabrahman'. The spirit (universal energy) embodied in the soul is that imperishable universal energy, which is beyond the illusions of space, time, and causation (karmas). The spirit remains one without the second but the individual soul entrapped within the body-mind nexus gets separated and conditioned by karmic laws. However, the spirit within the soul is an absolute part and parcel of the universal energy through which it continuously interacts internally as well as externally. Hence, when we say, 'Thou Art That,' we are merely indicating our true formless self, a part of that supreme energy, which is identifiable and identical to the Paramatma, i.e., God.

Since this subject is complex and unfortunately interwoven with many other branches of knowledge, there is a lot of confusion in understanding the basic tenets of the spirit, spiritualism, spirituality, and being spiritual. We are not left with many options but to blindly follow preachers, gurus, opinionated scriptures, and mythology jumbled with dogmas and rituals in precarious fables, concepts, and traditions, which only confuse us further.

In reality, there is no path that your mind can take towards enlightenment, liberation, or self-realization, for you are already that as an individual soul. What one truly requires is to declutter or liberate the mind from its rigid conditioning, which prejudices our thoughts in an imbalanced manner. Your soul, otherwise, remains identified and attached to the body, mind, and intellect. There is a desperate need to re-educate and renew the collective minds authentically towards what spiritualism advocates in Advaita Vedanta so that we may inwardly awaken our spirit rather than blindly follow those self-appointed spiritual gurus with fancy and exalted prefixes before their names.

Therefore, only after the spirit awakens, the mechanical mind is required to transcend in order to become aware and conscious of seeing this world with its third eye open. Please note, you are a composite of three elements—the body, which is guided by the mind, and the mind, in turn, is guided by the spirit, which is present within the soul. The energy to expand, evolve, effectuate, and excel within any brain does not require any prefix but only a suffix of -ness. The prefix betrays, meaning, you require a support for your personality to market your persona, whereas the suffix of -ness (refers to that mass noun) reflects the *intensity* of your eminence. Like in the case of aware energy or, say, how conscious you are, the suffix of -ness reflects upon the intensity of its presence. Like the intensity of the colour in a red rose is described from its suffix of red*ness* and not by adding any prefix, which are merely trophies meant to adorn something. For instance, a realized guru would never prefer to be called a guru, for he knows he is far beyond that.

The separation, which is created by the mind, chooses between this and that in duality, keeping your thoughtful self continuously dancing in the game of illusions. The mind is basically pivoted outward, forgetting and ignoring that there is a true inner self. This outer self comprises gross energy in the form of body and subtle as that of mind. As mentioned earlier, you never say or claim 'I am the body or the mind', you always say, '*My* body, *my* mind,' which indicates you are that conscious principle, which is above both. Meaning, this actual 'I' is more than body and mind. It is that core, the essential conscious criterion, which reveals who and what you are. Only after the body-mind is aware and conscious, you are considered to be mentally awake and alive. It is the presence of that eternal absolute aware energy (spirit) residing within the soul, which is the core seated within the mind, silently observing through the soul from that individual observer witnessing how the dual body/mind performs to experience life.

If we lucidly understand that the absolute energy is a unitary, continuous substance of everything, it becomes easier for the selfish mind to transform. The psychic energy emits a higher frequency, establishing better contact with the supreme energy to respond similarly. In short, the spirit is in everything, and everything is the spirit—one without a second. All observable particles of matter, when observed in their subatomic realm, spontaneously vibrate in pure waves of possibilities under different frequencies, even while interchanging from one to another—gases, liquids, and solids.

Meaning, the moment waves of energy manifest into a physical state of matter, it materializes into something for the period it exists. However, all that eternally exists is passively nothing but waves of aware energy, and this nothingness indicates non-existence in the form of quantum fields as probable waves of creative, dark energy. If we ask, 'What is the ultimate nature of this quantum vacuum of nothingness?' No one seems to know the answer. There are only concepts and opinions emerging from matter and consciousness for the period they exist, wherein we use God and devil as convenient factors.

Energy, by character, moves in a circle that has no beginning or end. Every end is the start of a new beginning. However, every cyclical movement also has a centre. This centre is the inertia of its centrifugal force, which creates a field. Likewise, the centre of life is its aware energy, which represents a centrifugal force creating a field of conscious orbiting to operate and experience the nature of dualities in polarities.

Similarly, the sun is that force of which light is its field. The ocean remains still and silent deep below its surface; however, ripples in the form of waves create a particular field from the intensity of its molecular vibrations. The sky represents that eternal, infinite absolute, but all that moves within its spheres—from seasons to clouds—are nothing but multiple fields of transient sub-energies within its domain. The centre represents that potential force from its absoluteness, which emits a kinetic field in various transient forms that gradually disappear, losing their quality while dispersing into the infinite zone of absoluteness or nothingness.

As an individual soul, you comprise of both—the thinking (personal) self and the witnessing (impersonal) self. The witnessing self embodies that presence of a force of aware energy, which radiates a field of consciousness symbolizing what you are as an experience-er of the inner and the outer world. Your centre (the force of energy) as the self-onlooker remains intact. Still, the field of self-consciousness expands and evolves in multitude ways only to gradually disappear in time, the way waves disappear in an ocean and the clouds disperse in the sky . . . into that infinite absolute expanse of the universe. Therefore, your mind has two directions to choose— either transcend towards that absolute centre of spiritual oneness or lose the nature of your true reality in that false material identification with a host of attachments. I prefer the middle path where I get the taste of both, with my third eye continuously open.

Even if you make sincere efforts to sustain in the centre, which is the oneness of all that exists, you will not be able to endure it for long. You may capture only glimpses of that centre, for short durations, because outward pressure from that centrifugal vibrating force will throw you back towards its field of operation, which you are supposed to experience in life. Thus, you—as an individual with a body, mind, and soul—have no option but to experience both: The divine and the devil, material and the spiritual, the real and the apparent, for that is what life is all about. However, in ignorance, we keep rotating unknowingly on the periphery, forgetting the spiritual centre, which creates a field of our karmic cycle in cause and effect to make our destiny.

The wise ones who are supposed to make us understand this simple truth either do not know, do not care, or do not wish to guide us on how to experience what this oneness of the ultimate self is all about. In the centre is that true Self, the freedom and the unity of its purity, where you do not require any outer god, guru, or any shallow personality. This centre of yours is that abode from where you originate and go back. This centre, if adequately understood, will enable us to experience all polarities concerning life effortlessly with our third eye open.

Therefore, always keep in mind, Pranayama is an exercise for the body, and meditation is an exercise for the mind. Whereas for spiritual growth, one just needs to be alert, attentive, and aware with the purpose of awakening that dormant spirit from moment to moment with effortless witnessing. It is required for that self-consciousness to transcend from the devil to the divine. You will continuously be alert and attentive, watch and witness from that centre—soul (inner self)—examine and experience in return who you truly are as that impersonal witnessing self.

The moment you renounce either the material or the spiritual, you start losing your balance. You become an egoist, losing the essence of what you are. You cannot renounce one polarity for another. What you need is to understand how to walk like a tightrope walker, balancing both ends of the pole in order to maintain that centre with grace and poise in a balanced manner. It is that judicious living experience, how to engage both polarities with the awareness that propels the required balance, where you learn how to live materially as well as spiritually, yet not identify or attach to any dual-factor out of the opposites.

The inner and the outer require your balance. You cannot eliminate any; you need to experience both to transform from the material towards the spiritual. Comforts for your body and equipoise for the mind are equally necessary to awaken that spirit sleeping within. Submerge yourself in both but do not get lost in either, and do not identify nor cling to any. The outer entity being the body-mind, and the inner subject being the soul are parts of the same whole. Without the presence of the devil, tell me, where is the need for any God? Unless you experience both, you will never understand life. They both go together, hand in glove, forming your whole or the totality of that Self.

Awareness consciously sedates the mind. You, as the individual presence of aware energy, cannot become aware because you are *already* a part of that awareness and are distinct from the sensory or thinking mind. It is the turn of the mind to become aware and for the thoughts to become conscious, awakening from their ignorance. You are that impersonal, impartial self within those illusions, which the mind experiences in ego-consciousness. It is for this reason, the sages claimed three basic states of the body and mind—waking, dreaming, and deep sleep.

You, as the presence of awareness, always remain aware in all the three situations, while the three states—waking, dreaming, and deep sleep—present in the body and mind come and go. The true self has only one state, that is of its being-ness in awakened awareness (Chaitanya). It is only through witnessing that the mind can awaken this quiescent self. It is like a movie theatre—the screen remains the same, but many films come and go. Similarly, the true self remains intact and is not affected, while the three mental states play their different roles of consciousness to appear and disappear.

To a sage, when the spirit is awake, the mind is dormant and vice versa, meaning, to be spiritual, your mind needs to be in silence. However, to the material, the thinking mind is essential. You need to quiet the mind, as far as possible, from various methods of spirituality, and, after that, you will need to learn and understand how to go beyond into the effortless zone of knowing the spirit . . . the presence of your true self.

I repeat, all mental efforts to practise and discipline the mind—whether vipassana or zen, yoga or transcendental meditation—may connect to the subject of spirituality, but they are performed and exercised by the brain under desire. These motivational methods can only take your mind towards the periphery, but the same mind cannot enter the spiritual zone, the centre. You are that centre, which requires only awakening from the mind. The mind is required to be in constant meditative awareness, alert and aware at all times— meaning, any efforts to practise meditation would be more of an exercise, endorsed and executed by the mind, for and of the mind.

A psychoanalytic interpretation of dreams claims that unconscious and unfulfilled emotional thoughts become alive during sleep. Whereas, spiritualists claim that your mind remains in a state of constant sleep, whether awake or in dreams, since it is functioning unconsciously from the subconscious level. Your mind continuously remains ignorant of your acts. Meaning, the mind mechanically functions in an auto mode from past awareness, and for this reason, it remains unconscious about the presence of your spirit. To a spiritualist, you are fully or partially awoken only after you are alert, attentive, and aware of your true hidden self in the present moment, and this is a state of least thoughts. Hence, an *awakened* soul functioning in consonance with body and mind are considered to be spiritual, also known as Chaitanya— awakened awareness.

So, who is present in those dreams? Science claims it can only be the mind, which thinks, dreams, and believes 'I am everything' along with the body. Therefore, according to the West, 'You are what you think.' However, according to the Hindus, whether the mind is awake, asleep, or dreaming, it is not the brain but the aware, conscious principle—the spirit/soul, which pronounces: 'I am, therefore, the mind thinks.' Hindus do not consider the operating system, meaning, the mind with its flow of unconscious thoughts to be that actual 'I'.

However, a true Vedantic would go further and claim that the body, mind, and consciousness—since all three are attached to the brain in duality—remain only partially awake in *unqualified consciousness*. A truly awakened person is that whose consciousness becomes fully qualified and is equal to awareness in *absoluteness*. In this case, the self-consciousness of the individual mind matures, qualifies, and realizes the true self in total awareness.

According to Advaita philosophy, all that exists is only a unitary pure and absolute aware energy, which is eternal, infinite, changeless, and timeless; neither takes birth nor dies. It is all-pervading, permeating, and penetrating the whole universe as the only existent. It is self-existent, self-aware, and self-contained, as it does not require any other form of energy to activate itself. It manifests in the human mind, which, in turn, becomes aware. This solitary self is neither awake nor sleeps or dreams. It is not aware of itself, remaining passive until it begins to vibrate and move. It is that absolute consisting of nothing and is called shunya. It is that potential force of energy, which manifests in its highest attribute only in a human mind.

The mind, if alert, is able to activate this potentiality through its power of intense observation in order to make it aware and, after that, through its attentive field of consciousness, experience life. From that nothing, it becomes something, which is everything for us. It is that initial state of observation, which influences and determines the nature of our physical reality.

In Advaita Vedanta, this state is called *Nirguna Brahman* or the Parabrahman. In consciousness, you may recognize this state as turiya. It is that state of fully qualified consciousness, where nothing remains, neither body nor mind, except total absolute awareness. However, it is challenging to realize this state while your mind is active and alive. Apart from that, the ego-mind persists, which wakes, dreams and sleeps, and falsely considers itself to be the 'I'. It cannot be factual because it keeps changing from one state to another; hence, it is apparent and illusory. The actual state of being, which is eternal and changeless is Parabrahman (total awareness), which neither wakes, dreams nor sleeps. It merely sees and witnesses through the mind without itself being the seer seeing the seen.

Dreams are nothing but reflections of our fanciful experiences. They cannot be taken separately or independently from our waking states. All three states reflect on each other— waking, dreaming, and sleeping. The only difference is that, in the wakeful state, your dreams imagine and fantasize externally about outer objects, and while sleeping, your mind dreams internally.

Chapter 14

THE POWER OF THE HUMAN MIND

*'The highest spiritual practice is self-observation
without judgment.'*
—Swami Kripalu

THE THEORY OF THE MIND WITH ITS PHENOMENA OF consciousness and qualia (the quality of perception) is, even today, disarrayed with confusion. Consciousness, the most fundamental essence and experience of life, which discloses physical reality, is not fully understood. Supposedly, if energy did not possess the attribute of awareness to make the mind conscious, then how can consciousness perceive matter to be solid? The brain on its own simply cannot do so while receiving electromagnetic impulses from the sense organs. There has to be another non-material substance to unravel all that we know. The mysterious subject of life is causeless and without any constraints from space and time, the only ultimate reality, which our sages referred to as the spirit.

It is the same mind, after being aware and conscious, which can postulate the existence of the universe—absorb, feel, think, and convert information to what it believes into personal knowledge, inducing and conducting further into actionable energy. The spirit is that power, which can develop a human mind into a limitless field of intelligence.

Therefore, the human mind possesses infinite potentiality; it has no limits to its expansion and evolvement, which is evident from the evolution that has taken place from the biological genus *Homo* to the modern thinking *Homo sapiens (wise man)* we comprehend today. The mind has the power to interact with the environment, forming thoughts into action from what it perceives. However, it remains unconscious unless the operator seated within awakens the spirit to make the mind aware and conscious of all that it sees, thinks, and does.

The subject of spiritualism tells us that awareness is that ignition, which is responsible for making the mind awake, alive, and conscious. The moment the mind independently observes, the spirit within that individual watcher awakens, igniting self-awakening (knowingness), witnessing the outer as well as the inner thoughts. All observable perceptions make the mind aware and only after that the mind is able to think and become conscious in order to develop the intensity of its self-awakening.

Meaning, the mind requires an observer to arrest and collapse the photons of light entering through the eyes to configure all those possible quantum particles arising from the wave function theory of energy into their actualities. The correlation of converting passive light energy from any possibility into its actuality by reinforcing constructive interference into an objective metaphysical reality is how I would explain the term spiritual awareness. Thereafter, at that very spontaneous moment, if the mind is attentive, it becomes proactively conscious of the same.

However, the moment it extends into the sphere of cognitive thoughts, consciousness emerges, and the mind separates every perception into dual from its absoluteness, consciously or subconsciously. It relates all that it perceives in duality in order to think, choose between the two, experience, infer, and realize, which we know as ego or self-consciousness. The message conveying the significance of awareness and consciousness revolving around one word 'witness' has been repeated time and again for the sake of clarity. Since the subject of spiritualism categorically revolves around awareness and consciousness, the connect to witnessing its own mind is straightforward and not attached in any frills and fancies to market fantasy and fables. The subject prima facie is more meant to understand clearly in order to know the subject of life with respect to its ultimate knowledge concerning the true self. Hence, repetitions are inevitable.

Therefore, we have two distinct selves embedded in our mind. The first is self-awareness, which emerges from the soul, and the second is self-consciousness, which emerges from ego. The unfortunate story of life is, most of us are not aware of its sublime relevance—the reason for all the chaos, depression, and misery in this world. *The presence of awareness is the awareness of that presence.* It is primarily that I-less state of self-awareness, which spirituality connotes as 'who you are'.

Now, self-consciousness is that subconscious mind (below the conscious section) presuming itself to be the lord and the almighty—a material disorder creating havoc in our collective minds without the world being aware of it. Spiritual awakening is to become self-aware of this illness to drop that self altogether into that oneness to which we all belong. To silence the mind into self-awareness, where the mind is centred towards the spirit rather than the material. In such a state of mind, the soul awakens, enabling the mind to become aware and conscious of the past, present, and future as one in totality.

In ego-consciousness, it is that feeling of want, which makes the psychic energy expand and evolve into a personal thinking self. Desire is that fuel, which makes the mind *move* to go on a roller-coaster ride of pleasure and pain. It is that want of the mind where if you get something, you are happy, otherwise not. Furthermore, want or desire brings the mind back to where it started, the *same point*, wanting something or the other, repetitiously. So long as the mind is active, there is desire; to live is a desire. It knows no end. Desires generate more desires because the fundamental nature of energy is to expand the moment it begins to vibrate and move. As long as there is a desire to live, the mind can never be desireless. After desire, it is hope that emerges to fulfil, enabling the mind to think, experience, choose, and infer. When the mind *identifies and clings* to desires, corresponding thoughts become anxious and imbalanced, inviting expectations and insecurity.

The brain exists; the mind does not. It is merely a flow of electromagnetic and chemical activity cruising through systematized circuits, comprising independent units. It transfers data from one section to another through neural pathways dedicated to various functions like memory, intellect, intelligence, recognition, attraction, vision, etc. However, desire is what makes the mind move; awareness is what activates the mind into action—spontaneous or otherwise—and consciousness is what makes the mind think in duality.

Desire is that energy, essential for the material world, which is the cause and effect of what we are. Just as the mind cannot separate from desire, the true self—the soul—cannot separate its link with the cosmos. Both cannot move without the other; they are interconnected. When the mind observes any object of attraction externally, desires naturally arise. Similarly, if the mind is alert, it witnesses what is happening inside out, meaning, its thoughts. In this manner, the true hidden self, the, soul awakens. Therefore, attachment to desire brings in grief, and simply being a witness to what the mind desires usher non-attachment—the key to spirituality—which drifts the mind away from identifying the dual element of attachment and detachment.

The mind remains *limited* if it is not self-aware. In such a state, the mind functions from its past knowledge, projecting that into the future with hope and desire, primarily, to satiate its selfish wants. Meaning, in self-consciousness, the mind subconsciously functions in an auto mode from its memory and intellect, recollecting past knowledge to advance and progress. Whereas in self-awareness, the mind is aware and conscious in the present moment, in the now, spontaneously infusing fresh, creative energy due to which all discoveries and inventions have taken place. When all three combine—past, present, and future—as one, the mind gains limitless intelligence, unfolding the unknown to be that known.

Furthermore, after comprehending the who and what the true self is, the brain becomes qualified to distinguish between the mind and the spirit. The subject of spiritualism directs the brain primarily towards self-knowledge, where you are required to understand the subject with clarity rather than merely absorbing what you read or what you are told. The spirit is basically the context of *who* you are, signifying the mind to be that content of its quality, summing up to *what* you are, contained in a body/brain, reflecting *how* you are at any given space and time.

Our ancient sages declared that wakefulness of a human mind is simply an illusion. In such a state, a human brain remains asleep in a dreamlike manner because of unconscious thoughts overly acting in a subconscious manner, emotionally thinking and imagining with desires and attachments. The mind goes wild with unpredictable changes of pleasure and pain. It awakens after it is stimulated from its conscious section (the spirit) to make the mind aware of its unconscious behaviour. When the superconscious area (soul), meaning, the spiritual section of the brain awakens, it merely *observes* the other two sections—conscious and the subconscious—while interacting with the mental self and the environment. It is only during this short period of observation that the mind is fully focused on what it sees, rather than analyze through thinking.

Observation is what makes the mind aware and, after that, conscious of what it has observed. It is during this short period of observation, awareness is absolute—thoughtless and choiceless. Meaning, after observing, when it extends further into the mind, thoughts emerge in duality either to function consciously or subconsciously to choose what it desires.

Therefore, when the mind is alert, observant, aware, and conscious, all three sections come together as one to make your mind function in a wholesome manner. You, as the impersonal witnessing self, awakens, and the personal thinking self, in turn, becomes secondary. Meaning, there are two minds—the witnessing mind and the thinking mind. The former resides in the superconscious section minus thoughts as the transpersonal witness—which we refer to as the soul— and the latter flows in the conscious and the subconscious part as the personal thinking self.

* * *

What do we mean by being spiritual?

To be spiritual means you, as the spirit, are not the seeker seeking, through mind, the sought because the thinker and the thought are the same. Where there is doership, consciousness is bound to the karmic laws. However, when you remain a mere spectator, an onlooker, you do not identify either with the witnessing consciousness or with the thinking consciousness (self). Unaffected and uninvolved, you, in such an awakened awareness, are not bound to any likes or dislikes, nor do you cling to any of this or that. Your mind is free from pleasure and pain, as well as not linked to past destiny, i.e., it is aware and conscious, but not attached.

To put it simply, when you surrender the ego mind, it dissolves, and you become spiritual. To be spiritual means you are neither the thinker, experiencer nor the enjoyer. Say, if you are driving a car—in spiritual terms—you are neither the driver nor a part of the body that is being driven. In fact, you are that essential *drive* or *observation*, which is the presence of aware energy, that being-ness, which is making the mind aware of the situation at hand. You are responsible for linking the observer (soul) observing through the mind on the object being observed.

You, as the spirit, are that silent observation, which requires no thinking or participation. The spirit merely observes without any constraints of space and time in the absolute, where there is no involvement, engagement, or contribution of any action by any doer doing the done. You are the noumenal presence, that knowingness, the individual intensity in abstract waves of aware energy, which never sleeps . . . that redness of the red or greenness of the green.

Though the words 'soul' and 'spirit' are used interchangeably, the primary distinction between the two is that the spirit is universal and the soul is individual. Soul is that highest indicator towards the spirit and that link between the mind and the cosmos. Being individualized, it is a grade less than the spirit. Soul is the realm of the *witness*, it is that true individual self, playing the role of a witness-er.

Please keep in mind, since the soul is not identified with the ego, it remains midway between the personal self and the transpersonal—the no-self spirit. However, after the death of body and mind, an individual soul, with no role to play, dissolves to merge into the universal spirit of aware energy. Meaning, the witness-er (self) has to die and collapse into the ultimate reality where there is no-self; the subject-object relationship between the individual and the cosmos ends with the soul. The I-ness merges with the I-less state of non-dual awareness as one.

In order to live a wholesome and fulfilled life, it is essential for us to know the true metaphysical self beyond the body and mind. It is difficult for the mind, through logical thinking, to understand with clarity this complex phenomenon of the self—the truth behind *who* and *what* you are. You are neither the body nor the mind because you can see your body changing from childhood to now, and you can feel and observe how and in what manner your mind thinks. In a dream, you also watch your body and mind going through all sorts of experiences while it is comfortably reclined on a bed, clearly indicating you are beyond.

You are the spirit, that being-ness, which knows in freedom of what it sees and not from its biased experiencing and enjoying, for that becomes personal, entangled in duality. Only a quiet (thoughtless) mind has the ability to watch and witness through its superconscious section of *what* you are in body and mind and *who* you are as the I-less state of aware energy in absoluteness. Hence, attaining self-knowledge is more of spiritual acumen rather than an intellectual assumption.

I repeat for the sake of clarity, you as that being-ness (spirit) remain as you are—absolute, pure, and total, the presence of abstract aware energy; thus, you are beyond the body, mind, and consciousness. You are a part of that universal aware energy, which prevails everywhere. Hence, the subject of spiritualism is to study that no-self through the self, and, in order to overlook the bodily self, the only way is to become one with the I-less state of nothingness. Meaning, the no-self state of being-ness in the form of self-knowledge with that personal thinking self. This visionary study reveals that unless *the individual soulful self liberates from all identifications and attachments (jivanmukti)* from its body and brain, it will not be able to realize the I-less state. Because of that, it becomes difficult for the thinking self to be truly one with that divine spirit. Therefore, while living, you may not realize total enlightenment or bliss, but you will definitely reach closer to this ultimate realization.

Furthermore, there is no substantiation or authentication to prove the continuation of the soul transmigrating or reincarnating from one life into another. In fact, the soul, as mentioned earlier, is that witness-er, which embodies the spirit. After death, the role of an individual soul ends, the witness subsides, and the spirit of awareness—which it embraces—goes back into the expanse of the universal spirit of energy.

Moreover, awareness, as I have mentioned multiple times, is that being-ness of who we are, the spirit, which unfolds all that a human being perceives of the universe: Aham Brahmasmi—I am that spiritual conscious energy . . . one without a second that never incarnates. Hence, the question of reincarnating does not arise. This spirit remains constant as it is, the way it is, eternally flowing, which has been well elaborated in the *Shanti Mantra* as well as in the law of conservation of energy. It is that absolute universal energy, complete on its own, with zero bindings to any matter or consciousness. It is the mind and the body that reincarnate through genetical transmigration from one life to another—attributable forces of the parents transferring from the mother to the offspring.

Therefore, when all knowledge ends, what remains is only the truth, *as it is*, requiring no intellectual interference. For truth cannot be arrived through experiences, it can materialize either from seeing or from understanding. Truth is that ultimate knowing from which everything becomes known. Hence, you are that truth, which requires no experiencing or explaining from the intellect. The spirit neither needs to become something nor requires self-realization or any sort of reincarnation.

Truth is inside everything existential, as it is, the way it is. Most of us do not wish to know the truth of who and what we are. Selfhood is an illusion; we are nothing but waves of probable energy because, in actuality, there are no selves at all. What exists in the subatomic level is only one in its oneness. You, as the metaphysical reality, are one with all, nothing else but the relative truth inside that absolute truth, which exists as it is, the way it is, in the eternal now.

Nobody is holding you responsible for your present karmas in your *next* life or sending you to heaven or hell. What you have is just the presentation of the noumenal spirit as waves of aware energy entrapped in an individual soul to counter and check multitude levels of consciousness in every phenomenal mind of a living creature. Therefore, you are responsible for this very life, so, face it and live it, and do not have any fears for the next. The continuity of the composition of what you are in this very life is reflected basically from the genetic mutation. Spiritually, the body, brain, and its mind are nothing but an illusion. They comprise a temporary combination of earth, water, fire, air, and space—five elements condensed into a triad of body, mind, and soul.

Karmic laws are basically bound to the mind with a cause and effect, combination of past actions to current reactions. Your personal life now is tied to the past from your previous developments and the genetic framework of your parents. Break this link in the present moment and create a new destiny for your future. Epigenetics and psychosomatic experiences will reveal you can make a lot of changes in your destiny from your present karmas. Self-consciousness or ego remains suppressed, subdued, and stifled in its 'me and mine' from constant desires of the mind, and in such reconstruction performs its samskaras—the subtle impressions of our past karmas. Thus, wake up and free that soul from your mental imprisonment to witness life from your spiritual realm. It shall make all the difference in that *Sanatana Dharma* (eternal righteousness) to which we are all ordained.

You, as the true eternal self, are free-flowing waves of aware energy presenting itself in particles of matter and streams of consciousness. An awakened and aware person is never aware of his or her own awakening; he or she makes no effort from his or her mind to know or let others know about his or her actual self-awareness. He or she has a certain aura by which others discover them. All attempts to show that you are somebody or something comes from the mind, the ego. Meaning, the brain only needs to become aware, not the actual 'you'.

Ego is present the moment you project yourself as somebody. Let us take the case of those gurus in our country who try to convince others of what they are through their branding, clothing, and personality, creating a falsity of projecting a godly mind. Moreover, there is no cause for a guru to add prefixes with attributive names of gods to demonstrate or substantiate as someone superior than his or her followers. Superiority radiates and reflects on its own; inferiority stresses and emphasizes. Blindly following a guru, a person (follower) loses his or her own power of intelligence and individuality; he or she tends to imitate, gossip, and repeat like a parrot what the preacher impresses upon his or her personality.

When your mind follows any ideology of a guru, master, or teacher, you as a thinker become an *intellectual* in that particular subject with borrowed knowledge. But this sort of knowledge will never be complete unless the mind becomes personally aware to consciously experience that individual level of one's own intelligence. Moreover, a true guru does not need to market himself or herself and create followers; he or she simply dissolves in oneness with his or her disciples as one and not two.

The mind basically functions on what it believes, so, be extremely careful before you begin to believe or follow someone. The spirit, on the other hand, merely *flows*— representing the presence of an individual intensity of awareness, observing and witnessing all that the mind sees. It makes the mind *instinctive, intelligent, and intuitive* to check on who and what the mind should believe and follow. Please keep in mind, the witnessing self (soul) within you is merely that watcher/witness-er, observing your body and mind of what it does to make your mind aware and conscious.

My dedication in this subject is to make you discover the nature of your true reality. It is to distinguish *you* from *your shadow*—the alter ego or that illusory self. I am, in no way, trying to imply that your second self should not become something. For it is not possible. Your becoming-ness (body-mind) in the physical form is equally important in this worldly life along with your being-ness in meta-physicality. So long the mind vibrates, ego shall prevail, there will be movement, and each body-mind will become something unique from all others.

Your body, mind, and soul shall depart from this life, but they will leave behind that individuality—a legacy of your past deeds—for others to remember when you are no longer there. So, be free to enjoy and celebrate this material self, just do not cling to it; always witness and be aware of it. Open your third eye. That is what life is all about, mechanical vibrations from body and mind to experience the relative dualities of life from its unique frequencies. But if the mind is constantly aware of the true self, it will be able to maintain peace and poise in order to fulfil life in its totality of body, mind, and soul conjoined as one.

My treatment of Vedanta rests upon one absolute reality in which there is no such thing as unreal; only the permanent and the real exists as not two. Hence, both the absolute and the relative, meaning, the non-dual and the dual, are one and intrinsically the same. The catch here is that when seen by the cognitive mind, it is finite; seeing from the soul, it becomes infinite. Thus, Brahman is both the transcendent as well as the immanent reality of all that exists in the universe. It is that innate source of gravity, electromagnetism, and all other interchangeable forms of subset energies. It is the ground and the unified field of energy, the totality of which remains constant as one without a second. The inherent nature in its highest attribute is referred to as Paramatma (awakened awareness) and the lowest as Jivatma (ego-self).

Out of one, the other appears for the duration that it exists to go back into the same. It is that one behind many, and is the one in all that exists as well. On its own, the spirit of awareness has no meaning remaining passive and dormant as dark energy. It requires duality to experience what life is about, at least, for the while that living matter exists. The spirit merely surfs between the material and the spiritual without any effort to allow the body and mind to become something unique while it is alive. Just witness that flow from your soul, the presence of your individual intensity of awareness surfing on its own. It does not wish to become something or change into somebody. You, as the unchanging spirit, are a part of that sky, which sees everything including your body and mind flowing like a transitory cloud in the expanse of its limitless potentiality.

To sum it up, spirit or aware energy is the centre of that transcendental force from which an immanent field of matter and consciousness appears to disappear. It is that noumenal from which all phenomena emerge. Being spiritual is to be persistently aware of who you are as a witness (Sakshi), making the mind, in turn, existentially conscious not to identify and attach to what you are.

Chapter 15

THE POWER OF THE HUMAN SPIRIT

'Desire and aversion are of the mind.
The mind is never yours.
You are free of its turmoil.
You are awareness itself,
Never changing.
Wherever you go,
Be Happy.'

—Paramahansa Yogananda, Ashtavakra Gita
(15.5)

THE WORD SPIRIT IN OUR SUBJECT RELATES TO THE declaration that we are more than body and mind. In body and mind, there is an observer, thinker, and doer, whereas spirit is that medium, the vital principle, which makes the above three acts possible for any doer. It is that abstract state, quality, and the metaphysical fact of being-ness from which everything arises and unfolds. Spirit is that which makes us awake and alive—the ground of our being—the infinite, formless substratum from which everything appears and disappears. Spirit is that truth beyond comprehension, which remains constant at all times, whereas the mind and consciousness keep changing within space and time. It is that awareness, which is always there, passive and potential, which never does anything but is responsible for everything done. Allow me to take you in depth into the study of this crucial element of our life, which most of us are ignorant of, as to how and why it is the true nature of reality.

The spirit is that constant force of abstract energy, which permeates everything available as passive aware energy within the transient brain, which, if awakened, merely watches and witnesses all that is around. It is that state of your being, and you are that, not the body or mind. This quality simply surfs between the material and the spiritual, binding the soul in karmic consciousness to experience a life of duality. We often synonymously use the spirit (Brahman) and the soul (Atman) as one and the same. However, even though the soul is an impersonal and impartial witness-er, detached from all mental activities, there is a distinct difference between the two. In the case of soul, we have a delicate subject-object relationship between the infinite *universal* spirit and the transitory *individual* soul. The soul radiates individually with the ability to make the mind aware and conscious. After the death of the body and brain, the role of the soul ends, the dualism in subject-object collapses and returns from its individuality into the eternal expanse of that universal ocean of non-dual awareness.

Spiritually, *you as that spirit*, remain a nobody and nothing, just being in the presence of cosmic energy penetrating, permeating, and prevailing in waves of formless energy, providing information to the soul without even knowing that you exist. The other *you as the personal self*, which is known by a name and gender within a body and mind, temporary subset forms of energy in matter and consciousness comprising what you are as the ego-self. It lasts for the period that you are awake and alive, which is more of an illusion in ignorance, not composed of any actual reality. Meaning, the true nature of your reality is that one source, one substance referred to as the spirit by spiritualism and energy by quantum physics.

Therefore, *who* you are is the spirit, which is considered to be quantum waves of cosmic energy. *What* you are consists of the mid-reality comprising the gross energy as body in the form of mind, and the core being that individualized intensity of aware energy encased in purity within an individual soul. In the ultimate reality, you merely compose of an intangible substrate of the spirit or absolute energy, the highest quality of which has been ascribed as the Parabrahman—total awareness from which the physical world appears and disappears.

In the philosophy of Hinduism (Sanatana Dharma—the eternal way), the most ancient religion known to humankind is a compelling affinity between quantum physics and what has been laid down by the concept of Brahman. Brahman is the essence of the universe, the ground of all being and that which surrounds and supports everything as the ultimate reality—a concept of Hinduism unique to this world. Many well-known physicists who pioneered the theory of quantum mechanics acknowledged and agreed to this similarity between the law of conservation of energy and Brahman—one source, one medium, the rest is all illusion. There were many who were inspired by the Vedic philosophy, like Erwin Schrödinger, Werner Heisenberg, J. Robert Oppenheimer, Niels Bohr, Carl Sagan, Nikola Tesla, and many more. According to Wikipedia:

> Brahman connotes the highest Universal Principle, the Ultimate Reality in the universe. In major schools of Hindu philosophy, it is the material, efficient, formal and final cause of all that exists. It is the pervasive, infinite, eternal truth and bliss which does not change, yet is the cause of all changes. Brahman as a metaphysical concept refers to the single binding unity behind diversity in all that exists in the universe.

The subject of spiritualism talks about the spirit (Brahman), apprising us on what it is all about. The body, mind, soul, and spirit are independent aspects entwined as one. Since they are distinct, their powers differ, but they support and sustain each other. The spirit embedded within the soul checks the mind, which directs the body. Spirituality, in turn, is the application or the objective of the subject of spiritualism while the spirit is undergoing a human experience. It is that reforming and disciplining experience for the mind involving efforts, practices, and techniques like yoga and meditation, which enable the body and mind to adjust, adapt, and amend from its random behaviour for furthering spiritual development.

The cognitive mind is everything for the material self but means nothing for the spiritual self, which merely witnesses those movements of thoughts flowing through many neural workstations of the brain. However, thought is essential to the mind, from which all feelings and deeds of happiness and sadness flow. Because of a host of multiple feelings, a psychological identity emerges and considers itself to be that 'I, me, and mine'. Since the mind has no existence of its own, it restricts itself to a name, gender, family, society, religion, etc., given by others. It continually remains insecure and under fear of losing its glory, and for this reason carries on accumulating and attaching to its false identity, always anxious for more and more. All thoughts relate to that insecure personal self, containing information from the past, and propelling that into the future. This is what the mind actually is, minus the spirit.

From the above, we assert the thinking psychological mind to be that personal self-embedded in a physical form of the brain and body. Besides the body and mind, most of us are ignorant of that third dimension, the subjective spirit—the source—which unfolds the universe and all that the mind configures. Otherwise, the mind functions mechanically, and because of this lack of knowledge about the spirit, it runs amok and creates havoc in most of our personal and physical life. If we wish to manage our mind from such anomalies, it is imperative we should know and understand, first, about the spirit, second, about the subject of spiritualism, and third, how to be spiritual. The Upanishads, the primary source on the subject of spiritualism, talk about the power of the spirit and the soul. How to open and free the mind effortlessly from its *finite* conditioning to its *infinite* cosmic expanse. It provides that clarity of self-knowledge from which everything becomes known.

The mind is an extraordinary operating system. It has *instinct*, which is pre-intellectual; *intuition*, which is beyond intellect; and *intelligence*, which combines both instinct and intuition towards the intellect to understand any situation from its own individual intensity of awareness. A thought, on the other hand, has no idea about its existentialism or what it is to exist. It depends totally upon past knowledge in order to project that into the future bypassing the present. The eternal now is that existential stage, from one moment to the next, which belongs to the exclusive domain of the spirit, in which there is no past, present, or future. It is that *presence*, where all three are conjoined into one without any constraint from space or time.

The mind has two distinct patterns of functioning. One is the *intellectual* where information is gathered from memory, desires, and karma (past actions), all three containing borrowed knowledge. A mind collects and subconsciously communicates the same through thoughts and language, projecting that into the future. Meaning, connecting past to its future for its selfish requirement—choosing, discriminating, experiencing, and realizing subconsciously or consciously . . . attached to dual thinking and relating in dichotomies for its self-preservation.

The other format for obtaining information is via *intelligence* created by flashes of fresh, spontaneous, and creative cosmic energy; pure and new making the mind self-aware in any present moment. In this case, thoughts are non-dual, choiceless; hence, not analytical, lasting for those fleeting moments before the mind extends into that evaluating thinking zone. It is this analytical zone, which separates the absoluteness of any informative energy in order to relate that with its opposite, to choose, experience, and infer. Both combine to form an image that has the power to intuit, imagine, think, experience, and infer in order to realize from its efforts. Please remember, the mind compulsorily requires to relate every form of energy to think and evaluate from its dual opposite. As a result, it separates the oneness of energy into two.

The specialty of thinking in every individual is that it has its own unique signature; the permutation and combination of each individual thinker differs from the collective intellect of any community. Meaning, all minds are distinct and unique in their own pattern of thinking. A mind, which can think, has thus been assigned as a thinker. A thinker is nothing but a summation of thoughts that always keeps altering within any space and time. Now, in order to think, the mind requires a conscious principle; meaning, consciousness to check the mechanical state of its functioning. However, for the mind to become conscious, it first needs to become aware, and that is where the role of the spirit commences. The spiritual aware energy is responsible to make the mind of any individual aware and, after that, extend to make the thoughts—conscious, subconscious, or superconscious—which is peremptory, in order for the mind to choose, experience, infer, and realize anything in life.

This book attempts to discover the secret behind the *power of the spirit*, the true zero-less self, which is distinct from that psychological self. It is that fundamental ground of existence, which is represented by its individual core consciousness, which we refer to as the soul. It is that third dimension, which, if not understood, makes the mind incomplete and unfulfilled to chatter recklessly and randomly, here and there, into this and that, for its likes and dislikes. It is that spirit of awareness, the knowing, which unfolds all that we know of this universe. So, who are you, not body and mind but the presence of that power—the knowingness, being-ness, essence, and quality of perception, which reveals that information— the universe is nothing but your own manifestation. Nothing exists outside of your being-ness, where there is no 'I' but only *that supreme energy*. Meaning, there is no 'me and mine' but only *us* representing 'all is one'—the presence of non-duality, the broad substratum as the foundation or the basis of duality.

Thus, the innate spirit enables the human mind to become aware and conscious, not only of the external world but also to *witness* all that is happening to its own body and mind. Spirit, with regards to our subject, is the highest attribute of absolute energy, which we refer to as Paramatma (beyond atma), signifying total awareness. It is not aware of its existence but has this ability to make the mind aware and conscious. It is that connection between the individual mind and the cosmos. Between the personal (ego) and the transpersonal (spirit), Antaratma or the soul is the individual home of that dormant absolute aware energy—the spirit embodying the witness. Soul is that individual witness-er, which on awakening within a human mind, radiates 'I Am That'.

Meaning, awareness is that force of spiritual power, which radiates a field of conscious energy in the form of an individual informatory centre. Furthermore, the soul or the witness-er is the highest indicator towards the spirit, and the ego submerged in its mechanical thoughts is the lowest. Both the soul and the ego survive in dual living within any individual with a subject-object relationship. Therefore, the being-ness within an individual is the aware energy, and the becoming-ness of one's individuality (consciousness) indicates through its experience of *uniqueness* of every living creature. Soul, I repeat, is that witness-er witnessing through mind on the witnessed object. After death, all three—body, mind, and soul—collapse into the universalism of the absolute energy of nothing—shunya—where there is no presence of any I-ness, the ultimate reality of who you truly are.

In this manner, the dormant, imprisoned spirit within an individual soul unquestioningly remains aloof and passive from those beliefs, desires, and emotions flowing through thoughts from the memory and intellect. Thoughts, primarily the subconscious ones, remain distant from the spirit. They survive and persist so long as a thinker identifies and clings to them. It sustains while the mind is active and alive, unless the inner spirit awakens to witness in order to make the mind shy and conscious of those unconscious thoughts—the mess and misery—which the mind subconsciously creates.

Spiritualism is a subject that speaks about the spirit, which is embedded in the brain but is distinct from thoughts. It enables us to understand the mind and not control, suppress, or rule it. It creates a gap between you, as the presence of that aware energy or spirit, and what you are in your psychic thoughts. When you watch and witness your mind, you are in spontaneous thoughtless awareness, without identifying with any belief, emotion, or desire. At this moment of now, you neither choose, condemn nor connect to any of your thoughts; you are merely allowing them to flow in the direction they wish. You, as the spirit, are separate from your thoughts behaving as the 'witnessing awareness'.

The subject relating to the power of the spirit (Brahman) is gradually becoming vital as more and more evidence is clarifying that, in the true nature of reality, there are no physical things. Quantum physics, which many of us do not bother to understand, is discovering when you smash particles of atoms in huge accelerators, they are not physical at all; everything at its fundamental level is one and only constant energy (Brahman). Meaning, the divination of Brahman, what the ancient sages declared millennia ago, is emerging to be true . . . all what objectively exists is only an illusion and we as humans live in ignorance.

The true nature of reality is one energy in unity and in continuity, which is subtly aware. It responds to and corresponds with the information that the brain receives and interprets through a state of consciousness called reality. We are connected with each other as one force and field of energy, which we spiritually refer to as awareness and consciousness. The reality, which we physically observe, perceive, and experience expanding through our senses occur merely as appearances on a macro level (Brahman—to expand and grow) from the micro levels of its highest attribute, interfacing awareness and consciousness as one. The true energetic nature of reality prevails within an unchanging quantum field as pure waves of energy, better understood as intelligence, information, instinct, intuition, spirit, energy, witness, life, and God.

Now, in order to be spiritual, the mind needs to be alert to watch and witness impartially, on its own, without identifying or attaching to any of its thoughts. The reason, all thoughts are conditioned in some way or another through centuries of past pronouncements, proclamations, or precepts turning you into a zombie functioning subconsciously based upon beliefs. It remains a prejudiced follower of other's experiences and knowledge, not bothering to utilize its own personal intelligence. It performs like a mechanical computer through its memory and intellect with borrowed knowledge from its past data, only to decode and decrypt nothing new or afresh. This is all because the mind remains ignorant of the spirit or that divine intelligence residing within.

So, if you wish to discover a realm beyond the efforts and methods of spirituality, you will need to go beyond intellectuality and the mind's realm of experiencing under motivational practices in transcendental meditation or physical tenets of yoga. The subject of the spirit bestows that innate knowing from the intensity of its aware energy providing the correct answer to what life is all about, not only scientifically but spiritually, too. It requires deep intelligence to recognize and understand this power, which differs from the intellect one possesses. You need to be a serious seeker to study this subject independently, and not have biased opinions because of other source of subjects like science, religion, psychology, or any other mental mix-ups.

You will find many knowledgeable people who claim to be spiritual because they have read some books or follow certain gurus. However, there is no guarantee that they *understand* the basics of what the spirit is all about or what it means to 'be spiritual'. Intelligence is required to lucidly understand what the mind perceives and cognizes. Otherwise, if it is just from intellect, the mind becomes bound to blindly follow something or the other, believing what others narrate—either from exhausted scriptures or through past accumulated knowledge—not caring to understand the same from its actual authenticity. For this reason, intellectuals become scholars, and scientists are innovative through their intelligence.

The mind as we know flows and revolves around the 'I' factor, always expecting and wanting something or the other for its material self. It is that small 'i', which denotes the personal self, constituting what we call ego. In fact, both ego and thoughts basically constitute the mind. The smaller part of the 'I' factor connects with your rational thinking through thoughts, emotions, and desires. As mentioned earlier, it is called the intellect, which is the faculty of reasoning, objectively deciding on all matters of external cognition. It creates that personal, separated 'you'. The big 'I' is considered to be that soul, the witnessing self or that potential divine, residing within. Let us see what this 'I' factor is all about and where does it derive its power from?

In spiritual terms, body and mind are not that 'you' but your mind thinking it *is* you; it is that ego (thinking self) in self-consciousness. It is definitely *yours* but not *you*. It is derived from borrowed accumulated knowledge, which you have gathered over time from here and there, or what others have provided in the form of name, gender, beliefs, and what and whom to listen and follow. It is devoid of any freshness. This part is responsible for forming your superficial personality, a false 'persona', which develops an intellectual identity to inflate your ego further. The small 'i' survives on past and future thoughts always bypassing the present. It is for this reason in spirituality, the intellectual mind is considered to be always asleep. It has all the knowledge that the mind subconsciously remembers through thoughts from memory and determines from the intellect. It merely oscillates between the two polar ends of any duality—relating, distinguishing, and discriminating one from another. In such a performance, the true spiritual 'I' plays no role.

The spiritual 'I' emerges from total intelligence, the presence of that individual intensity of aware energy. Intelligence is that degree of cleverness arising out of alertness in every living creature. It prescribes to that *quality*, whereas intellect subscribes to the *quantity*, which an individual mind retains within itself. Intellect comes from others, but intelligence is your actuality—the presence of your aware energy; the spirit subtly disclosing the essence of your uniqueness. It prevails and expresses spontaneously only in the present moment and gradually fades when you become a follower and start to emulate others. It captures instantaneously, combining pre, present, and post, i.e., information to present something new that is responsible for forming your uniqueness out of those billions of people who survive on this earth. It is immediate, spontaneous, and proactive in its formation and does not feel or react emotionally in any manner. Fundamentally, it is that inner intensity of spiritual awareness—*the unique intelligence*—which is the qualitative 'you' and not that quantitative 'what you are' that you intellectually borrow and memorize from here and there.

Intelligence is always free and fresh, springing forth for you to understand something, and not from what you already know or gather. It provides you with that intrinsic quality to apprehend any knowledge in its right perspective. It is not bound to any part of your cognition. Intellect, on the other hand, is constrained to prior knowledge gathered over time and depends on memory. Intellect discriminates, believes, determines, and concludes, whereas intelligence doubts and questions from the intensity of its aware individual energy.

The second 'I' is *instinct*. It is proactive and responds to a particular stimulus before the mind can initiate its analytical thinking. It is more biological because the stimulus activates an impulse in the entire body and mind. It is that gut feeling. This inactive section of your mind is not dependent on memory, intellect, logic, reasoning, thoughts, or even consciousness. It is a flash of natural intelligence, which reveals your innate self. Instinct is natural, intellect is analytical, and wakeful instinct is the spirit that activates your mind to become aware and, after that, conscious.

There is a third 'I'—*intuition*. It is the ability to know and understand anything without availing any support from thoughts or reasoning. Instinct and intuition are interchangeable and combine to give you the spiritual intelligence that knows far beyond your cognitive mind. It occurs when your spirit is awake. It has no prejudices or distortions of the cognitive mind, and it is referred to as a hunch or the sixth sense.

Instinct, intuition, and intelligence are the three sentinels that emerge from the silent levels of the limitless, unconscious mind. They collectively form the 'third eye', which has that spiritual power through its wakeful innate intelligence to simply watch and witness, providing fresh energy or awareness to the alert and attentive conscious mind. Soul energy has a direct connection with cosmic intelligence since it is absolute and beyond the thinking mind. The presence of this energy in the superconscious part is what makes your mind alive. Spiritually, this universal 'I' has been referred to as the actual presence of 'who you are'. We are all spiritual beings going through human experiences, but social conditioning, imitating others, blind beliefs, strong desires, and ignorance about the presence of this spirit deter the development and growth of this spiritual 'I'.

The fourth 'I' is the state of your inner consistency, which reveals your *integrity*, forming the sum total of your character and consciousness—intelligence and intellect combined.

It is the totality of your cumulative *intentions*, showing the degree of your wholeness or fullness for any situation or circumstance. It actively emphasizes on the evolution of your consciousness holistically.

In the new era of artificial intelligence (AI), what we have is a trending technology that is soon expected to surpass the intellectual domain of the human mind. According to various scientists, if the human brain can function in an auto mode through its subconscious level, then why can't robots with artificial intelligence do the same? For the first time in the history of humankind, we have AI touching upon the essence of the human intellect, but in no way can it come closer to the unique spiritual intelligence that being-ness, which we all individually possess. Unless, of course, if they, too, devise a method to connect with the cosmic energy.

Meaning, the human mind will still reign supreme due to its 'I' factors like instinct, intuition, and that combined unique intelligence from which everything becomes clear and transparent. This section of the brain has been ascribed to that sphere in which the spirit resides as that 'witnessing self'. It has the ability to perceive beyond cognition levels of the conscious and the subconscious since it is prior to thinking in duality by the mind. Science may succeed in replicating the human mind through, what it calls, artificial intelligence, but it cannot duplicate the spirit, which is that unique 'you' in the form of aware energy, responsible for arousing and activating the *finite* mind to the expanse of the *infinite* cosmic intelligence.

In a nutshell, spiritualism is all about the wholesomeness of the spirit or that universal energy, which is aware and claims that you are not the thinker, seeker, doer, experiencer, or the enjoyer. These are mere different dimensions of the cognitive mind. Furthermore, meditation, yoga, t'ai chi, Zen, etc., are mental or cognitive methods to practise for the sake of disciplining, silencing, and transcending the mind towards its actual spiritual self.

It is only in the absence of thinking that the spirit awakens. The spirit within is already that transcendent in the presence of intense waves of pure aware energy, which requires no further operative methods or disciplining from the mind. It is the realized, enlightened divine that makes the mind aware and conscious of countering and checking the random behaviour of thoughts. The spirit does not participate or perform in any activity; it only watches and witnesses, monitoring the mind to make it aware and conscious. Spirit is that pure and total aware energy, absolute and non-dual, which the mind separates relating everything in duality to experience and realize what life is all about.

Chapter 16

THE SUPERCONSCIOUS MIND

'If you wish to be free,
Know you are the Self,
The witness of all these,
The heart of awareness.
Set your body aside,
Sit in your own awareness.
You will at once be happy,
Forever still,
Forever free . . .
You are everywhere,
Forever free . . .
If you think you are free,
You are free.
If you think you are bound,
You are bound . . .
Meditate on the Self.
One without two,
Exalted awareness.'
—Thomas Byron, The Heart of Awareness a
translation of The Ashtavakra Gita (1.4–14)

WE NORMALLY CONFUSE BETWEEN THE MEANINGS OF
spiritualism and spirituality and take them to be the same.
Spirituality discusses more on the application of the subject

to attune the mind towards the spirit. It has a lot to do with methods and practices of how to discipline the mind. Therefore, we should first try to find the meaning behind the word spirit, which will make us understand about its philosophy and the role played by the spirit in our material life. Unlike other subjects, we have multiple interpretations to apprehend this branch of knowledge. Moreover, since we are not required to provide any evidence, it is left on the seeker to decide what he or she wishes to agree and understand. All my books are primarily concerned, first, with knowing about our true self in order to understand with clarity: How to be spiritual?

As mentioned before, spirituality is that mental exploration on the subject of spirit. When the mind is silent, the spirit awakens. The process to silence the mind is what we call spirituality. Through its flow of thought, the mind unconsciously demands and questions and answers for its expansion, evolvement, and effectuation, multitasking into this or that for its likes and dislikes, randomly and recklessly. As a result, perception and apprehension are one-sided and overly dependent on the subconscious level functioning in an auto mode from the memory and intellect. You, as the spirit, remain dormant because your mind, being ignorant about the true self, remains overwhelmed with ego, immersed in its 'me and mine', presuming the false self to be its actual reality.

Therefore, methods like meditation, yoga, religious practices, etc., which are generally practiced to still and discipline the mind, remain inadequate, bouncing back with vigour to its original ego-self. The moment the mind, after meditating, concludes, the ego-thinking self returns with double strength to gossip, 'Oh, you know, I am meditating these days!' Subconsciously, the memory remains convinced and presumes: *I am that something who is one step ahead of the other.* The spirit requires no practise of any sort but sheer awakening, and for that, you are just required to effortlessly make the mind alert, attentive, aware, and conscious. You cannot invoke this state of mind by any mythical, mystical, or rehearsed techniques, nor can you induce any mental efforts or methods.

Moreover, if you have noticed, it is futile to discipline, suppress, or control the mind. It bounces back to its original framework. We have no option but to go beyond cognition and enter into the zone of the superconscious mind—unconscious section to the western world—to awaken and kindle the spirit. To enter this superconscious state, we first need to know and understand the mind inside out, which is extensively discussed in this book. It provides us with the ability to get a grip on our true self, which is beyond cognition, and consequently, be able to know the difference between the physical self, the thinking self, and the spiritual self.

Spiritual knowledge takes us beyond the physical body and brain to what quantum physics claims today that physical reality is an optical illusion (Lila) and everything at the subatomic level is nothing but waves of energy. Meaning, all that fundamentally exists is the one and only constant energy manifesting itself in different forms. It also states that unless there is an observer to observe, there is no physical reality; implying, energy becomes aware when there is consciousness to observe.

Let us go deeper into these waves of energy from the spiritual aspect: a) body—the physical self b) mind—the thinking self c) soul—the witnessing/observing self d) spirit—the being-ness or flow of awareness (spirit). The mind that thinks is nothing else but thought. Who is conscious of those thoughts flowing in the mind? The witness-er (soul). For anything to appear in your mind in the form of thoughts, someone needs to make the mind aware in order to make it conscious to think, experience, and infer in the manner the mind desires. Meaning, spiritual intelligence (awareness) is that universal self, whereas the individual observing self is that soul, and the mind is that thinking self, basically an operating system functioning mechanically in autopilot like a computer. Therefore, until the mind becomes aware and conscious, meaning, without an individual observer (soul), the mind can neither be aware and conscious nor feel, think, or experience anything.

Awareness is there in all sorts of acquired perception; it is the basis of all knowing. Knowing is the base of all knowledge, and through knowledge, we happen to know what existence is. So, the foundation for all knowledge and existence is awareness; after that, we are required to be conscious of what we are aware of in order to experience. Moreover, without an observation, mind cannot be aware, and without being aware, there can be no consciousness. Thus, the brain is nothing but an information processor through its mind, a set of neural networks transferring information from one section to another where neurons get activated by *spiritual awareness* to know what we know. Hence, we are the subject as a witness/observation, and the nature of our reality is in its being-ness or awareness.

Now comes the part of the spirit and how does it differ from the soul (observer/witness-er)? Simple! You require a participant, a self to observe. Meaning, for an observer to observe is more of an act for which you require an individual doer. A doer, we know, will normally be biased while observing, wherever the mind is focused and engaged, seeking a selfish outcome. It is always goal-oriented, like an eagle hunting for its prey. There is a separation between the seeker and the sought . . . a duality. However, in the case of the spirit, it merely remains as the witness, free from any doership in total awareness. Therefore, the witness is the subject (you) and the witness-er is that object witnessing through the mind of what you are.

Therefore, even though the soul is impersonal and impartial, there still remains a duality between the cosmos and the individual. There is a subject-object relationship between the universal spirit and the soul, the personal and the transpersonal. Soul is the abode of the witness (spirit).

However, after death, the soul collapses and the spirit inside merges into its universal field. Witness is that testimony, uninvolved and unaffected, whereas the observer (soul) is focused and goal-oriented; like a tiger hunting for its prey.

Therefore, observation/witness is merely a flow of energy—passive and dormant—a state of a non-doing. It is that presence of pure witness designated as being-ness without seeking any outcome—choiceless and thoughtless. Whereas, I repeat for the sake of clarity, the soul is that individual witness-er and the mind is that operator busy in witnessing, thinking, and doing. The mind is an organizing processor that is continuously regulating its psychological energy in electromagnetic chemical activity from its mental faculties. In the game of life, you are the *origin*, the spirit within that soul, which is silently witnessing through the mind its manifestation, and the mind is *what* you are in quantum—identified and emotionally attached to a name, gender, and what not!

After that comes the difference between the observer and the observed. We need to first keep in mind that the observer is only a part of the subject of the observation or witness. Therefore, please do not get confused here by presuming that the observer (witness-er) is the same as observation (witness). The observer is a doer, and the witness merely materializes. The observer, I reiterate, is only a part of the observation (spirit).

However, when all three conjoin, they disappear from their independent status, and what is left behind in totality is solely the presence of the witness (spirit). Meaning, when the mind is witnessing the flow of thoughts without seeking or thinking independently. It is not constrained from any space, time, and causation; it is merely observing without any judgement or discrimination. The mind is, then, not involved and, in this case, the witness witnessing the witnessed, becomes one remaining pure and absolute in its observation without the interference of any brain and body.

Under normal circumstances, the mind predominantly functions in duality, relating to its opposites to choose one out of the two, experience, and infer. The likes and dislikes choose on that observation in preferences with a certain want. However, the witness, the presence of waves of energy, quietly watches and only after that the neural pathways in the mind get initiated to separate the absoluteness of every energy in duality. Meaning, even in this case of separation, where each is playing a separate role, thought (mind) still remains as awareness, so does the thinker (ego) as well as the observer (soul). It's just that all the three function with a lower intensity or frequency of awareness.

However, in a state of excellence referred to as self-realization, the witnessing self (soul) becomes *one* with the witness, free from doership in pure consciousness, where you remain totally uninvolved and unaffected. The soul is, then, not bound to any identity or attachment—being in the world as well as outside this world. The actual meaning of 'the witnessing consciousness' (Sakshi) becoming one with the spirit (Chaitanya). The mind is silent and the spirit is awakened.

Please note that continually witnessing in totality during physical life indicates the one who has attained self-realization. He or she as the witness-er has now qualified and effectuated the true I-less nature of being the witness in totality. The body and mind of such a person perform all actions but are not bound to any name, gender, or attachment. In this sort of excellence with total awareness, one remains a witness to all that he or she does, yet remains free from doership, uninvolved and unaffected through a tranquil mind. The difference here is that all actions take place, and you are not bound to any of those doings.

Mind is a mere presentation of *what* you are; you are the source and mind is that transient manifestation of what you wish to see, feel, think, and experience what life is. Mind, through its consciousness, *reflects* the state or the intensity of your awareness. Only when there is synchrony between the intensity of the individual inner awareness with the outer universal energy, you are at peace. Meaning, the nearer the mind approaches towards the true self, it realizes oneness. The further away it is from the soul, the thinking self may attain profits, comforts, and pleasure but will also attract mess and misery.

So long there remains a separation between the observer and the observed, illusion prevails. You, as the witness, remain asleep from this world in a concept devised by the mind as 'me and mine'. Not admitting or realizing that there is no such postulation of *many-ness* in actual reality, but merely the oneness, which science refers to as energy, and in our subject as the spirit.

Therefore, you need to keep in mind that 'you' (the universal spirit or self) are that universal absolute, non-dual oneness in a state of I-less-ness– a witness. The individual self—presuming to be the 'I am' devised by the thinking self—is a misnomer, especially when you consider mind and its thoughts more to be yours as a possession. Mind is what it believes to be based on an external persona, comprising abilities and ambitions within that energetic aura of its individual knowledge and information, which we refer to as the thinking self. The observer or the witness-er, I repeat, is that individual aware consciousness, a potential intensity of awareness, performing the role of a witness within an individual soul. It remains dormant due to the mind continuously separating everything in its false me and mine, immersed in desires and attachments.

The witness, please remember, is grounded in the soul. It is simply another aspect of the spirit. However, when the soul gets disconnected with the body and mind, after death, the role of the witness is over, and the dualism of subject-object ends. What, then, remains is only that infinite expanse of absolute non-dual awareness—the ultimate reality of everything that permeates this universe. The spirit is that *noumenon* of all perceptions from which all phenomena appear and disappear. The interlace between the non-dual and the dual. The clouds disappear and what remains is only the sky.

The soul is always free, impartially witnessing all it witnesses, neither involved nor affected in any way, remaining just an onlooker to what has occurred. It is the nearest benchmark to the spirit, yet radiates only in an individual, whereas the spirit illumines universally in everything. Hence, when the witness-er (subject) and the witnessed (object) dissolve into one, what remains is only the presence of that witness in fullness—YOU. The universal subject is that witness (a feature of the spirit) residing in every individual soul (observer), and the nature of that witness is to make the mind aware and, after that, conscious, while the observer, observing through the mind, is creating its own objective reality from the observed.

Both witnessing and thinking are different. In the former, the flow of energy is absolute, non-dual, and it is the subject; whereas in the latter, thoughts are always dual and objective, concerned with a certain want for the outcome of its efforts. In the former, you are an onlooker, merely a watcher; and in the latter a participant. We normally witness in a wrong manner, more out of judging and evaluating rather than purely as a witness with no-mind and no-thought. The moment a thought emerges, we have ripples of vibrations in our consciousness.

However, when the mind is still and quiet, witnessing is creative and fully aware. Also remember, thoughts (mind) can be inwardly witnessed by the witness-er (soul), but the witness (you as the spirit) can never witness itself. This is where the difference lies between *who* as witness/spirit and *what* being the triad of the body, mind, and soul. Witness is like a mirror, many come in front, watch, and go, but the mirror remains the same. Thus, you as a witness/spirit, are like that mirror, which flows beyond the triad of the body, mind, and soul.

Furthermore, there is also a difference between witnessing outside and witnessing one's own body and mind. Inner witnessing, even with closed eyes, creates self-discovery, enhancing self-awakening in subjectivity. Outside witnessing is considered as seeing, noticing, and observing with your eyes open, creating a certain self-observable reality—the observer effect. Nonetheless, in spiritual terms, inner witnessing is to go beyond observation, without concern for any outcome in order to become one in absoluteness with what is being witnessed, without the perceptual senses playing any role.

Witness with no-thought and no-mind is that one word, which summarizes the whole subject of spiritualism and was first put forward and stressed by Sage Ashtavakra millenniums ago during the Vedantic period. We are normally accustomed to converting everything that we see and observe into a thought. However, while thoughts are passing by in your brain, try and witness those thoughts in total silence with no idea, postulation, or comment; pure inner experience with no involvement from the mind. Be yourself, remove that mask of your personality from your mind—from name and gender to everything given by others. Disengage and witness spontaneously in purity. Mind, instead of reacting analytically from its false 'me and mine', will pro-act and your individuality will reflect its true colours in totality, free from any bindings to this or that in likes and dislikes.

Spiritually, you are meant to be spontaneous in every act. You go deep into that unconscious section of the mind, which is untouched by the conscious or the subconscious thoughts, away from the memory and intellect. It is that third eye or the sixth sense in total silence, which only watches and witnesses to make your mind aware and conscious. I refer to this section as the superconscious part of the mind that connects to the infinite cosmic expanse. Justifying that bold statement, our ancient sages declared 'Thou Art That—Shivohum'. It means the true self (soul) in its original, pure, and primordial state is identifiable to the ultimate non-dual spirit or the absolute energy in its totality as one. Thus, remaining as a witness, the mind will be free from all the entanglements it identifies and attaches with. When you are away from that thinking self, you are neither the seeker, knower, believer, doer, enjoyer nor the experiencer. You are merely a witness of all that body and mind engages, experiences, and effectuates. We refer to such a sublime state as being spiritual.

The mind has greatly evolved over a period of time, reproducing data on what it perceives through its senses from the outer world as well as the inner consciousness. Spirituality shows us to discipline the mind experientially, how to enhance its awareness following certain practices like meditation, chanting, breathing exercises, and praying to pursue ceremonial and conventional rituals. When all these come to an end, spiritualism begins.

Hinduism is a deep spiritual philosophy originating from the six schools of Sanatana Dharma, accepting the Vedas as an authoritative source of knowledge, which conveys that God and soul are one and not distinct from one another by further claiming that the Creator and the creation is one. Meaning, soul is that individual part of that universal Brahman, which contains the highest attribute—Parabrahman. This indicates knowing oneself is equal to knowing that God within oneself. Soul is that spiritual principal, the breath of life, the essence of individual knowing, the silent indweller performing as the observer/witness-er of all material beings. The moment you go beyond the personal soul, you dissolve into the transpersonal state of being-ness, waves of pure, absolute non-dual energy.

Soul is the endmost understanding of what you are providing the doctrine about the end of all knowledge. It is from this knowing that everything becomes known—all that exists is *not two*. However, terms like the spirit, spiritual, soul, etc., are expressed very loosely, where they enter from one ear and go out of the other without anyone bothering to comprehend the complexity behind the essence of these words. Even today the soul remains a mystery to science since no one has the patience or inclination to know thyself. Therefore, I suggest, one should be cautious and serious before entering into the subject of life or, for that matter, reading a book like this one.

The mind *generates* and *constructs* consciousness, and all three—body, mind, and soul—collapse when the body and brain die. However, the same mind, when the brain is alive, receives cosmic energy, like a mobile phone receives signals directly from the satellite. Meaning, every individual soul connects with the cosmos and is between the personal (ego) and the transpersonal spirit. The true self, the subject of what we are, is validated more as the soul rather than the objective thinking ego-self.

The soul signifies the role of an impartial witness. It merely watches the mind, which, in turn, after being witnessed, becomes aware and conscious. Watching, witnessing, or observing generally happens spontaneously in absoluteness; it is only after cognization that the mind takes over to think, and the process of duality begins. In our case, the spirit is the witness and the soul represents an individual observer, observing through the mind on the object being observed. In witness, there is pure oneness—the observer, observing the observed are one. It is the mind that separates the absolute energy after observing to feel, think, analyze, choose, experience, and realize the observed object for its self-interest.

Therefore, awareness or the spirit exists independently outside the cognitive mind and is beyond the limitations of space and time. It is present everywhere, non-local, inside (soul), and outside (cosmos) of the brain. It is for this reason the spirit, being pure and totally aware, is considered to be that absolute, independent, and eternal . . . distinct from the mind. It only watches and witnesses from within the superconscious section of the mind where no thinking prevails, allowing the brain to become aware and conscious of what it performs.

The role of this operating system pronounced as mind is bound by space and time. This neural process is required by the brain to compute data from its past inputs after extracting from its memory, configuring and catapulting that into the future, and bypassing the present. However, the said mechanical operation comes to life, or switches on, only after the soul awakens to make the mind aware and conscious. Alert, aware, and being attentive are the three switches that awaken the soul, empowering the mind to be aware in the present moment of what it perceives—inwards or outwards. It is the intensity of individual aware energy, that being-ness, which comes to the rescue of the mind, differentiating it from any mechanical operation.

This absolute energy is present in every existential moment. It is a part of that infinite, eternal presence of potential universal energy, which is responsible for making the mind pro-act at times, spontaneously, without reacting in any thinking of the past or wanting something in the future. In this manner, the mind becomes a composite unit to utilize past, present, and future as one.

Embedded within the brain, this individual presence of aware energy becomes the source representing 'who you are', the potential force responsible for creating its field of operation in the form of consciousness. It remains dormant, unless alerted by the mind. I repeat, if the mind is alert while watching and witnessing, it awakens that inert spirit immersed within a soul. It becomes responsible to make the mind, first, aware and, after that, radiate in its field of consciousness. Witnessing this higher self play the role of a soul forming a certain degree of uniqueness, playing a game of duality with its lower self in ego-consciousness, integrating the higher to the lower, creating an individuality, reflects the intensity of 'what you are'.

Allow these two to play their roles independently. If you wish to be free from the mess and misery the human mind has created for the material self—in the course of providing technology, money, power, and fame—the price we have to pay for all the advances and comforts has become all the more imperative. We surely need to balance that with spiritual means in higher consciousness. If you wish for mental peace, grace, and tranquillity, you have no option but to be free from all identifications and attachments, and yet be able to utilize the same during the course of your mind operating in the circle of duality. Hence, the level of consciousness in each individual reflects from the quality of self-awakening depending on its nature of experiencing from the conscious (aware self), subconscious (thinking self), and the superconscious (the witnessing self), which the mind goes through during its psychological and physiological life.

The subconscious state of mind is that reservoir in the form of memory, forming 'what' you are as the 'rememberer'. Since the mind mostly functions from the subconscious section in an auto mode from the memory and intellect, it becomes emotionally bound to ego with a name, gender, and identification—continuously demanding all that the mind unconsciously and mechanically desires. The conscious section represents the field, or the individual *quantity* of aware energy, and the superconscious section expresses the force or the individual *quality* of aware energy, presenting itself as the true observer of *what* you are within the human brain.

Both the conscious and superconscious sections determine the level of your self-consciousness, whether it is flowing towards the divine or the devil. Therefore, consciousness presents itself in three different attributes—the first two behave in the form of consciously or subconsciously behaving in the mind. Besides that, we have the third functioning independently as the witnessing consciousness originating from the superconscious, overseen by the flow of witness, representing the actual *who* you are in absolute awareness, that, too, in a realm of no-mind, no-thought, impersonal, and impartially signifying 'That Art Thou'.

Awareness is that force that guides the field of psychic operations spontaneously or consciously checking while the brain is actively operating and boosting its mechanical CPU, the mind. It makes the mind subconsciously or consciously aware of deleting all those excess files the brain carries from its reckless and restless thinking, choosing from its past and future thoughts during its existence. It has two distinct attributes, first, as spontaneous awareness, which remains absolute and creative, proacting with choiceless thoughts on any situation. Secondly, the moment awareness extends into the cognitive mind, awareness radiates a field of self-consciousness, where thoughts become aware and conscious of the information and knowledge it receives from all over.

A choiceless thought is pure and uncontaminated, effortlessly operating in the present moment, gradually deleting all viruses from the mind. Whereas an unconscious thought with extended or past awareness materializes mechanically out of desire for any feeling based from its past data. Subconsciously thinking, mind detects, discriminates, and determines any sensation relating to its opposite in order to experience and realize its material requirements. All thoughts originate from the past and project that into the future. The unique signature, which every individual mind reflects, comprises fundamentally either out of the conscious or from the subconscious state of mind.

The superconscious mind is merely the observer, which influences what the mind observes, deriving its awareness from the cosmic cloud of aware energy. Approximately 95 per cent of the mind's functioning is done unconsciously at the subconscious level, approximately 4 per cent by the conscious and the remaining 1 per cent by the superconscious. I repeat, spirit is that aware energy, which turns on the ignition, making the mind active and alive from its frozen state. Mind becomes aware and responds in a superconscious manner, *proactively* in choiceless thoughts to any stimulus or *reactively* thinking emotionally either consciously or subconsciously.

The human mind is a complex operating system embedded in a physical brain and the relationship between the two is far from understood. Science is still not confident enough to answer why we are awake, aware, and alive or how do we experience sensations? It depends mostly on assumptions provided by philosophical concepts. Spiritualism conveys that thoughts flow in the manner the mind desires. However, keep watching and witnessing these thoughts while they randomly flow in your mind. Do not create any obstructions in its path or be bound to any of its identifications or attachments. It is an uncontrollable mechanism; love, pamper, and take care of your mind. Witnessing inwards will automatically make your mind shy and aware as well as conscious of all its mechanical functioning, enabling you to determine and decide which proper direction to follow.

Mind is highly rebellious. It prefers to function on its own, without any interference from your witnessing or intellectual self. The more you attempt to tell the mind to not feel, desire, think, or do something, the more it rebels with extra vigour. Therefore, do not obstruct, hinder, or stand in the way of the mind. It is a phenomenal machine; allow it to flow the way it wishes. You may alter, divert, distract, expand, evolve, or transform the mind, but you can never control it for too long. All you can do is watch and witness, be aware and become conscious of what your mind is doing on its own. Make all attempts to become a *watcher* of your own mind rather than be that knower, thinker, experiencer, or enjoyer of the mind.

Consciousness may curb and discipline the mind for a while through yoga, mantra, and tantra but, then again, the subconscious takes over, and you get lost in your unconscious thoughts originating from the memory—'me and mine'. Say, you begin to start learning something—driving, swimming, or meditating—at first, your mind is aware and conscious, but gradually, all functions are taken over by the subconscious to manage on its own, unconsciously. The conscious section goes to sleep, and the subconscious takes over. The subconscious directly connects with the memory and the intellect retrieving its data as and when the mind requires, consuming over 95 per cent of all psychic activities. It is vital for the material world, being fast and furious . . . multitasking here and there, reason for which the western world considers the power of the subconscious to be that ultimate. However, the subconscious mind is responsible for creating most imbalances in your life, certifying the way you have progressed materially but regressed spiritually.

Conscious thoughts are slow and defined, which your mind has chosen over other ideas for any particular moment. The conscious mind commands and the subconscious follows. Like, when you start to drive a car, the mind is alert and focused, consciously concentrating and giving directions for its destination; gradually, the subconscious takes over, not requiring any further consciousness. After that, your thoughts drift to other factors simultaneously thinking into this or that. However, behind all this activity, there is another watcher *who* silently observes what the mind does. It is that degree of *observation* or that *drive* (awareness), which oversees through its *observer* (soul), the functioning of the mind. It is that presence of *who you are*—a silent self—voicing its opinion in a soft, subtle manner whenever you cross any limits.

Memories are triggered by neural pathways stored throughout the brain and are used by the entire mind. Consciousness is something remembered from the past, reminding you of what the mind wishes to know, which also includes remembering your name and gender. When the mind becomes conscious of any sensation, it objectively thinks in a focused manner. It understands, identifies, compares, analyzes, and discriminates between any two relative objects. It is slow because it can think one thought at a time, choosing what it desires inwardly or outwardly. What it opts for, consciously, is always in duality, opposites of, say, positive/negative, good/bad, etc., for self-gratification.

As mentioned earlier, consciousness from the thinking self is that experiential quanta of what, why, and how you are. It is that remember-er who figures out what your mind is watching and has become aware of internally as well as externally. It is the sum total of your past awareness. It is more of a culmination and content of your past conscious experiences in the formation of determining 'what you are'. Self-consciousness comprises primarily those internal reflections in the mind from its thoughts. It is unique in every individual. You enter the conscious portion when the mind is attentive, adding to its ability the power of the intellect to differentiate between two perceptions. In both the conscious and subconscious stages, the mind has to rely on its past data to take you into the future.

Superconsciousness, on the other hand, is the fountainhead of the actual 'who you are'. It is your third eye, between the eyebrows. It is that spiritual centre that draws instantaneous cosmic energy to manifest in the mind as awareness. It is responsible for your instincts, intuition, and intelligence and goes beyond the conscious and the subconscious. It is that creative eureka, the sixth sense, which is beyond the cognitive mind's capacity. The alertness divulged by the superconscious stage is the sphere of any present moment. It is that pure and simple witnessing stage where no thinker, thinking of any thoughts, is required. It is that still, silent, and serene mind observing and witnessing any situation where the mind has the master key to take you in any direction. This stage completes the mind's working from the past, present, and future as one. It is that meditative wholesome state where no efforts are required. It is purely existential and full of aliveness. It is proactive, spontaneous, and immediate without allowing the thoughts to interfere and analyze. It is that spirit of who you are.

The mind is thoughtless when it independently watches and witnesses in a state of self-observance, which is responsible for making itself aware and conscious. This sort of spontaneous flow emerges from the superconscious section, which our sages referred to as the spirit or that divine residing within: 'That Art Thou'. It is that distinct and absolute level of the mind, which does not think or participate on its own. It neither discriminates or chooses nor determines what the mind wishes for. It simply watches the mind, and that itself is more than enough to keep the mind in its rightful place. The mind is that software of the electromagnetic chemical activity occurring in the brain. Similarly, the soul containing the spirit is also a part of the mind; it is seated within only to watch and witness its own thoughts communicating internally and externally and is directly connected to the heart as well.

The only way you can awaken the spirit or that inner divine is by activating your superconscious section, developing and enhancing the habit of being alert. When you are alert, you merely watch and witness to become aware. After your mind is aware, it attentively extends further into thoughts and enjoins with memory and intellect, making it conscious. After this initial conscious stage, memory and intellect take over, making the mind function in an autopilot mode. This is called the subconscious grandstand where your presence of awareness is no longer required. This is when the mind, which is a storehouse of all your emotions and desires, *reacts* from past experiences.

You are already aware of the first two levels—the conscious and the subconscious. This volume emphasizes more upon the superconscious state, ignored state of the mind, which you critically require to usher a holistic balance in your life. The superconscious has the power of a supercomputer. Being the source of all creativity, it is responsible for providing you with limitless, unique impulses of intelligence, instinct, and intuition. It provides flashes of insights or those eureka moments, which all scientists, composers, writers, and artists unthinkingly and spontaneously attain when they go beyond the capacity of their cognitive intellectual minds. Superconscious energy gives the mind that extra boost to discover futuristic discoveries and innovations; people get ideas that are far beyond their intellect.

Therefore, the superconscious mind is nothing but pure creativity when your mind is alert and aware and focused on any object. This state of mind is above the other two states; it occurs when the mind functions in total meditative silence without your knowing about it. Like, if you go to sleep with a problem, this section of the mind works on its own and, invariably, has the answer ready for you the next morning. In spiritual terminology, we refer to this state as the sixth sense or the third eye.

Therefore, watching and witnessing the inner thinking self, submerged in its thoughts, is the highest activity of the superconscious section of the mind. When you are alert, you are fully awake and, after that, when you observe, the superconscious section gets activated. It is an *effortless* state of meditative awareness where thoughts are silent during those moments. It is at this moment that the cosmic energy from the outside spontaneously manifests into your mind. Silent and effortless meditation is what we refer to as constant 'witnessing' of all that is around with a still mind.

The first step occurs when the mind is alert; it makes the mind observant. In the second step, the observant mind becomes aware, and the third is the consequence of awareness where the mind becomes conscious. The fourth step occurs when awareness extends into the cognitive realm of thinking in duality; it subconsciously takes over the psychic engine in ego-consciousness and, subsequently, the thinking self takes over the reign to become the active operator demanding all the credit for its illusory—me and mine. In this state, the mind functions unconsciously from its subconscious section, without referring to the conscious or the superconscious extent for any of its requirements.

Let us again recapitulate. During the first stage of superconsciousness, there are flashes of absolute non-dual perception with immediate awareness. In this state, the mind is most creative. Your mind at this stage, unquestionably and unconditionally, pro-acts and does not react. It is neither thinking nor emotionally desiring anything. We refer to this section as the potential divine awakened within. The second stage commences with extended awareness, filtered by the mind through its attentive thinking in duality of what the sensory organs perceive. This extended awareness makes the mind consciously perceive via thoughts of what it is observing.

The third stage occurs when the mind subconsciously thinks, chooses, and determines from its memory and intellect how it wishes to react from its past awareness. In this case, the mind is in an auto mode and performs all its activities without any support from the other two sections.

Let us take an example to understand this process better. Say, you are watching and observing a beautiful flower and are captivated by its sheer beauty and fragrance. During that moment of enchantment, you are fully immersed without any analytical thoughts and are one with the flower in absolute awareness. After that, the second step begins, this awareness enters into your discernible and tangible cognition, thinking starts, and your mind becomes aware and conscious. It starts to dissect, compare, and analyze all the parts of that flower and its flora—from photosynthesis to pollination. A spiritualist, say, will be struck with awe merely admiring its beauty and fragrance in totality, whereas a materialist will compare, analyze, and dissect its beauty, tearing it into fragments for its personal use.

I repeat, when you plainly watch, you merely observe. During that present moment, you do not change anything. You as the subject and the flower as the object under observation are *one* in total awareness for that existential moment. It is only when your mind becomes conscious, it begins to compare; meaning, the primordial awareness has extended, and the thinking self now becomes conscious to separate the unity of one into two. While you were observing, beauty was there, you were connected; now in thoughts, you have become aloof, a *separation* has been created between you and the object. The subsequent steps subconsciously follow—you might discard it, break it into pieces, or place it somewhere and soon forget about it. Therefore, so long as you observe, your relationship is one in totality. When awareness continues, the mind begins to seek something for itself, and while discriminating, a separation emerges, you choose and determine in self-interest. This is how conflicts between 'mine and yours' arise where every individual mind believes something different from another.

The spiritual state of every human mind demands more of meditative awareness in the present moment, and existential and spontaneous remembrance from one moment to the next. In this state, the mind is alert and attentive in every moment for any duration—pure and still—an I-less state of being-ness in totality. Sigmund Freud was the first to discover the conscious, subconscious, and the unknown unconscious sections of the mind. Later, another section was found by Carl Gustav Jung, which he called 'the collective unconscious mind'. However, long before these discoveries were made, the Hindus had declared the third unknown section to be that divine, the third eye of the superconscious mind.

Acknowledgements

I WISH TO EXPRESS MY GRATITUDE TO ALL:

My friends who helped with their critical analysis throughout the gradual progress of this book and my editors —Sonali Pawar in India and Julie Oughton in UK—who went through the manuscript time and again, adding their inputs, and revealing it as it is today, substantially enriching the final result.

A deep and heartfelt appreciation to my family—my wife, Komilla, who patiently overlooks my distracted nature while I am busy penning my thoughts, and my daughters, Nadisha and Shreeya, who are my greatest critics.

I am forever grateful to my late parents who laid the foundation of my scientific and pragmatic nature.

Notes and References

1. A mantra that reminds us of our oneness with the absolute, the transcendent, the ultimate reality—the truth.
2. In physics, the observer effect is the disturbance of an observed system by the act of observation. This is often the result of instruments that alter the state of what they measure in some manner.

About the Author

GIAN KUMAR was born into a traditional Hindu family in Burma (present-day Myanmar). From childhood, his life held paradoxes which he struggled to understand. While he was educated at a Christian boarding school which observed strict religious practices, these were diametrically opposed to the Hindu traditions and customs which were the norm when he went home for the holidays. A thinker by nature, the inherent confusion and dogmas underlying religion gradually impelled him towards spirituality. Gian hopes to share his own experiential learnings with others through the medium of his books. He lives with his family in New Delhi. www.giankumar.com

HAY HOUSE
Look within

Join the conversation about latest products, events, exclusive offers and more.

f   Hay House

 @HayHouseUK

 @hayhouseuk

We'd love to hear from you!